THE WIGAN JUNCTION RAILWAYS

By

Dennis Sweeney

TRIANGLE

PUBLISHING

Copyright © D.J.Sweeney 2013.
First Published 2013 by Triangle Publishing.
British Library Catalogue in Publication Data.
Sweeney D.J.
The Wigan Junction Railways
ISBN 978-09550030-5-9
Printed by The Amadeus Press Ltd, Cleckheaton.
Written, compiled and edited by D.J.Sweeney.
Cover design by Scene, Design & Print Ltd, Standish.
Designed and Published by
Triangle Publishing,
509 Wigan Road,
Leigh, Lancs. WN7 5HN.

Front cover. The scene at Wigan Central on 21st September 1963. The occasion is the Locomotive Club of Great Britain's 'The South Lancashire Limited Railtour' worked by Stanier class '8F' No.48178. The train waits to depart for the Bickershaw Branch and Pennington Junctions to Kenyon Junction. Further Details of this tour will be found on Page 114. *John Ryan.*

Rear cover. Fairburn 2-6-4T No.42063 crosses over George Stephenson's Liverpool-Manchester line at Kenyon with a Manchester Central-Wigan Central service on 29th July 1963. *N.Dyckhoff.*

All rights reserved. No part of this publication may be reproduced in any shape or form or by any means electrical, digital, mechanical, photographed, photocopied, e-mailed or stored in any retrieval system without prior written consent of the Author and/or Triangle Publishing.

Plate 1. Manchester Central, the terminus for trains from Wigan Central as 'A5' 4-6-2T No.69822 waits for departure time in June 1958. These engines were introduced by Robinson in 1911, this particular engine being withdrawn in 1959.
W.D.Cooper, Cooperline.

CONTENTS

	Page
Introduction & Acknowledgements	4
The Wigan Junction Railways	5
Glazebrook	15
Newchurch Halt and Risley ROF	20
Culcheth	23
Lowton St. Mary's	31
Plank Lane	41
Bickershaw & Abram	62
Strangeways & Hindley	73
Lower Ince to Darlington Street	85
Wigan Central	103
Bibliography & Abbreviations	127

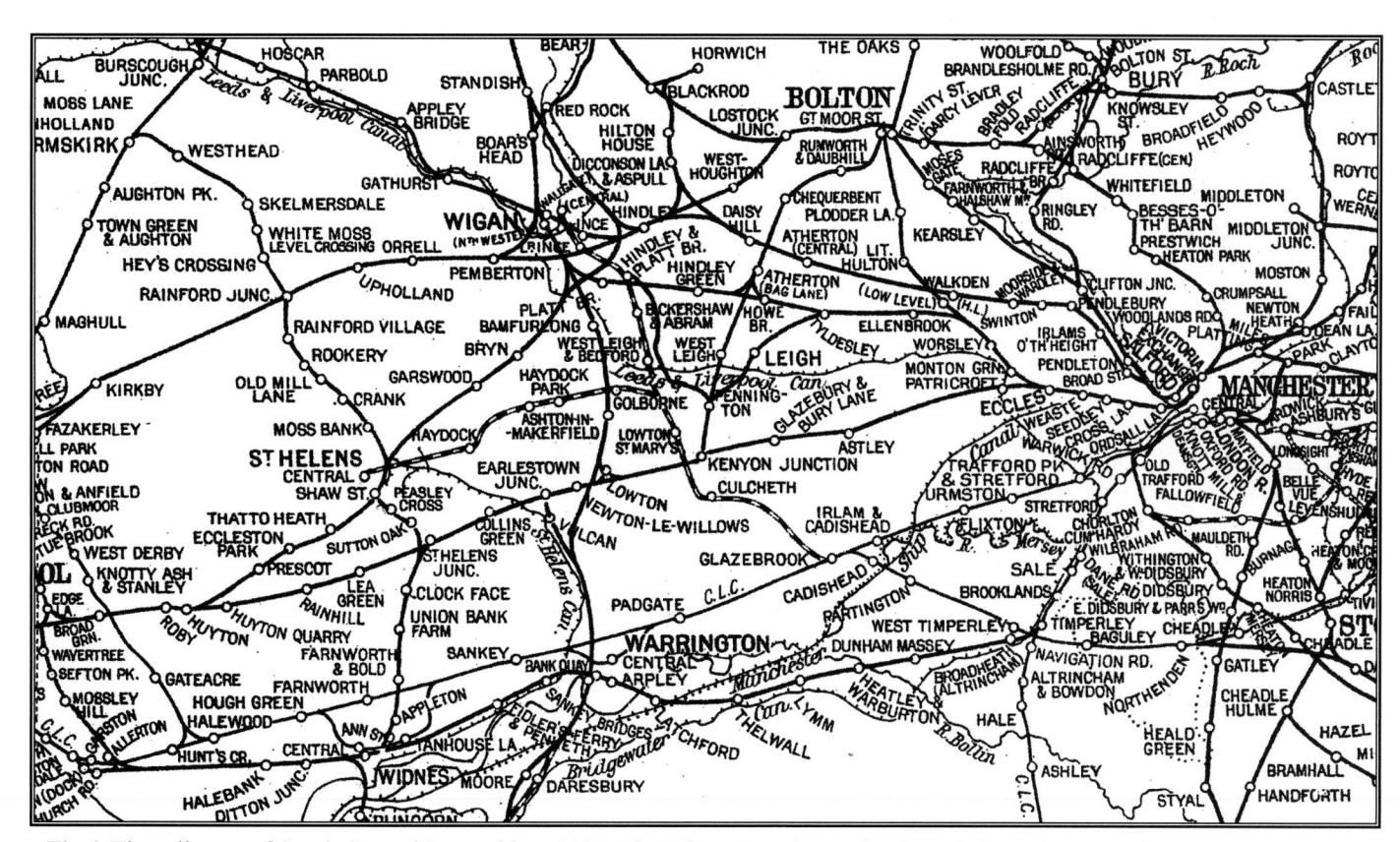

Fig 1. The railways of South Central Lancashire c1927. The Wigan Junction and Wigan & St. Helens Junction Railways are shown as broken lines
Courtesy, John Ryan.

INTRODUCTION & ACKNOWLEDGEMENTS

The prime intention of the Wigan Junction Railways proposals was to tap into the extensive coalfields of Wigan and the surrounding areas. In this they were supported by elements of the Cheshire Lines Committee (C.L.C.) with which railway the Wigan Company would make a connection at Glazebrook.

Chronologically, the Wigan Junction Railways were late arrivals on the South Lancashire railway scene, the London & North Western having a complete stranglehold of the St. Helens area and the lion's share at Wigan; even the nominally independent, coal owner inspired, Lancashire Union Railway had the backing of, and was worked by the London & North Western. The Lancashire & Yorkshire Railway was also well established at Wigan by its Manchester to Liverpool and Southport routes.

Canal operators were also very active in Wigan long before the railways arrived, and often a problematic competitor to them. Indeed, Wigan coal proprietors had been shipping coal via the River Douglas to the Ribble Estuary by 1720, and when the Wigan Branch Railway began constructing their Springs Branch line in the 1830s, found the canal authorities very protective of their interests to the point of being obstructive. One might wonder, therefore, what possible service could a railway latecomer hope to provide.

It will be seen from the map of South Lancashire's Railways on Page 8 that the area was already crossed by an extensive rail network and few major works were carried out in the locality after the arrival of the Wigan Junction Railways. The conversion of the Ackers-Whitley narrow gauge railway to standard gauge, and its extensions to Bickershaw and Pennington Junctions by the London & North Western in 1881, were a direct counter to the Wigan Junction route. The Pennington avoiding lines opened in 1903 gave more operational flexibility. Two major works carried out by the Lancashire & Yorkshire Railway were the Bolton avoiding route from Brindle Heath to Crows Nest, Hindley, and their Wigan avoiding line from Hindley No.2 Junction to Pemberton Junction.

Yet, it was the avowed aim of the Wigan Junction Railways, not only to reach Wigan but also expand to Preston, the Fylde Coast and beyond. The very fact that Wigan, one of the giants of Lancashire industry, was so built up it was to cost the interlopers dearly; so much so, that financially they were never able to fulfill their future plans.

Nevertheless, after a shaky beginning when revenues were not even covering operating costs the Wigan Junction Railways, and its descendent companies, were able to siphon off lucrative coal traffic from under the noses of the established railways as new mines opened up, in particular those alongside the Wigan Junction Railways between Plank Lane and Hindley. Some of these were to continue in production well into the nationalised era.

However, like many other branch lines in the post-war nationalised era its days were numbered as freight traffic haemorrhaged to road competition. Coal traffic had suffered from mining closures for some years and continued to do so, although some mines continued in production up to the mid 1960s.

I must express my sincere thanks to Gerry Bent, John Sloane, Alan Hart, Eddie Bellass, Ian Isherwood Dr.J.G.Blears, Tim Oldfield, Peter Eckersley and Michael Back who have provided so much material for inclusion. John Ryan has searched through his own personal archives to provide a number of illuminating sidings schedules and related documents.

Once again I acknowledge the experience of Bill Paxford, Peter Hampson, Tim Oldfield and Tony Graham whose knowledge of signalling matters has, once again, been second to none.

To the staff at Wigan & Leigh Archives, and Preston Records Office, I gratefully acknowledge the assistance so readily given.

For the industrial railway scene I have again relied heavily on the works of C.H.A. Townley, J.Peden, & Co., supplemented by my personal correspondences with C.H.A.Townley who provided so much information particularly with regard to the Wigan Coal & Iron Co. and their predecessors.

I have been greatly assisted with the unenviable task of proofreading by Gordon Rigby and Ian Pilkington and mere words are inadequate to express my relief at such assistance being so readily offered.

Lastly, to all of those too numerous to mention who have provided snippets of information and photographs, and to those who responded to requests in local newspapers for specific staff information, I express my sincere thanks.

At the time of writing, a volume covering the branch to St. Helens from Lowton is well advanced. This will follow in due course.

All scales and dimensions are given in Imperial Measure.
D.J.Sweeney, Leigh, 2013.

THE WIGAN JUNCTION RAILWAYS

The Wigan Junction Railways was first proposed in 1873, the necessary Parliamentary powers for its construction obtained in the Acts for 1874/5. The purpose of the railway, said its promoters, was to provide additional accommodation for Wigan and the surrounding areas, the prime object being to tap into the southern section of the Wigan Coalfield in the neighbourhoods of Platt Bridge, Abram, Bickershaw, Hindley and Westleigh, from a connection off the Cheshire Lines Railway at Glazebrook, thereby gaining access to the route of the constituent companies of the Cheshire Lines Committee, namely, the Great Northern, Manchester Sheffield & Lincolnshire, and Midland Railways. In the event, the Great Northern Railway effectively withdrew from the project having already spent a considerable sum of money constructing extensions in the Liverpool area which had yet to give any meaningful return.

Plate 2. Here, at Irlam Station, the workmen's trains from Wigan which served the nearby steelworks terminated. This view was taken about 1935. In the distance a train crosses the Manchester Ship Canal. *Author's Collection.*

The 1873 proposal envisaged a branch line running in a northerly direction from Glazebrook, to Wigan. The terminus was to be at Queen Street, adjacent to the North Union Station, whose lines it would have to cross by an overbridge at Ince, south of the Leeds-Liverpool Canal, with a short extension to Pottery Lane (Road). There would be a connection with the Ackers-Whitley branch line at Bickershaw, two spurs to the Lancashire Union at Amberswood and a spur to the Springs Branch. The Bill was therefore presented to Parliament by the remaining C.L.C. constituents.

As was to be expected, this was opposed by the London & North Western Railway. The Lancashire & Yorkshire Railway showing some solidarity with Euston, also objected to the plans. A number of private business owners, who perhaps saw an opportunity to extract greater compensation from the Wigan Company, also opposed the scheme. The London & North Western in particular objected to the proposed terminus in Queen Street, which they said, would interfere with the sighting of signals at their North Union Station.

Parliamentary approval was given to the proposal and the Act for construction received Royal Assent on 16th July 1874 at its first attempt. However, Railway No.1 of the Act, the main line from Glazebrook to Queen Street, Wigan was not allowed beyond the Leeds-Liverpool Canal at Ince, and the extension to Pottery Lane was also thrown out. Railway No.2, the spur at Plank Lane to the Ackers-

Whitley private railway at Bickershaw, and a short extension of it to James Diggle's Colliery by the same junction with Railway No.1 was allowed, as were Railways Nos. 3 & 4, spurs to the Lancashire Union Railway at Amberswood and Railway No.5, a connection at Ince to the Springs Branch.

Chairman of the Wigan Junction Railways was Mr Nathaniel Eckersley, M.P. for Wigan at the time. The other Directors were:- James Burrows of Wigan; John Stone of Huyton; James Henry Johnson of Southport and Samuel Thompson of Lancaster. The appointed Secretary was John S.Darlington and the appointed Engineer was R.S.Norris with Charles Sacre as Consultant. Norris was succeeded by C.H.Beloe in August 1876.

The Company opened an office in King Street, Wigan but the first Board Meeting of 15th January 1875 was somewhat of a farce as the Directors did not attend in sufficient numbers to form a quorum. Some three weeks later, an Extraordinary Meeting took place to discuss a new Bill for amending and extending the railway. At this juncture, the engineer, Norris, was instructed to take trial borings on Glazebrook Moss in order to estimate foundation costs. He was also to liaise with Wigan Town Council regarding works in the built-up area of the town.

On 2nd August 1875, a further Act authorised a station in Standishgate, Wigan, near the junction of Standishgate and Crompton Street. This was Railway A of the Act, and would run from a point 6 chains north of the Lancashire Union Railway at Amberswood where it would connect with Railway No.1 of the 1874 Act, and terminate at No.33 Standishgate, a distance of 2 miles 55 yards. Railway B of the 1875 Act, an extension from the terminus at Standishgate to connect with the Wigan Coal & Iron Company's Railway near Ryland's Sidings was not allowed.

Railway C, a branch connection from a point 1 chain north of Ince Green Lane, from Railway A, was to run west to Parson's Meadow Bridge where a connection was envisaged with the Winstanley Colliery Railway. It actually terminated in a field owned by Nathaniel Eckersley! From Winstanley, this colliery railway passed over the River Douglas at Parson's Meadow to a wharf on the Leeds-Liverpool Canal at Wigan - Wigan Pier! Yet another attempt by the Wigan Junction Railways to tap into the established coalfields of Wigan.

Another new proposal was Railway D, a branch from Wigshaw Lane at Culcheth to Padgate on the C.L.C Manchester-Warrington route. Both of these proposals were allowed.

Railway E of the 1875 Act was a new branch from Plank Lane to the Wigan Coal & Iron Company's Railway at Westleigh. It would begin at 30 chains north of the centreline of the Wigan Junction Railways bridge over the Leeds-Liverpool Canal, Leigh Branch, and running in a north easterly direction, make a connection with the colliery railway 3 chains west of Westleigh Lane at Fox Robin Fold. This too received Parliamentary approval.

Also allowed was a deviation of Railway No.1 of the 1874 Act, which would begin at Plank Lane, and running northwards for a length of 2 miles to a point where Railway No.1 approached the spurs to the Lancashire Union at Amberswood, with a maximum deviation of approximately 1 furlong at Bickershaw Lane. Further, Railway No.1 was to be abandoned 6 chains north of the Lancashire Union, at the same point where Railway A would begin and the levels to Railways 3 & 4 at Amberswood, and to Railway 5 at Ince, all of the 1874 Act, were to be altered to effect suitable junctions with the proposed Railway A, or deviated Railway No1. The branch to Diggle's Colliery from Plank Lane, Railway 2 of the 1874 Act, was also abandoned at this time. It seems extremely likely that Railway No.1, as originally laid out, would interfere with the future operations of the Moss Hall Colliery Company's mines at Low Hall, hence the deviation.

A total of nine contractors tendered for the Glazebrook - Hindley section, £110,000 being the lowest. In the event, that of Thomas & Robert Stone of Newton-Le-Willows for £120,498 was accepted, though this excluded foundation works over Glazebrook Moss. Thomas Stone had a £5,000 shareholding in the Wigan Junction Railway, not surprising then that their tender was successful. The estimate was later revised to £122, 678 but to include foundation work between Glazebrook and Culcheth.

The Chairman of the Midland Railway suggested that they, and the Manchester, Sheffield & Lincolnshire Railway, should take over the Wigan Company and build the line but the view of Sir Edward Watkin of the former prevailed, in that it should be left to the original promoters. Having completed all the test borings and legalities by September 1876, the first 'sod' was cut at Ince Green Lane, Wigan, on 27th October inst. by the Home Secretary, R.A.Cross.

It was soon evident, however, that the contract price was being exceeded.

From the main Liverpool to Manchester Cheshire lines route at Glazebrook West Junction, the Wigan Junction Railways proceeded across Glazebrook Moss where considerable difficulties ensued in the excavations for the railway, the contractor having to dig down to a great depth in order to ensure an adequate foundation with extensive drainage being required. Glazebrook Moss is an extension of Chat Moss which, some fifty years earlier had tested George Stephenson's skills in building his pioneering railway across the treacherous bog. In the twentieth century, construction of the M62 Motorway still presented the engineers with problems across the same area as the heavy machinery engaged on such a project often became bogged down in the mire and just to bring matters up to date, the present electrification of Stephenson's route is presenting problems with the erection of masts over Chat Moss, engineers having to sink piles 60ft deep to support them.

By March 1877, Thomas & Robert Stone had spent in excess of £160,000, and at the half-year meeting of 28th September 1877 held, according to the *Manchester Guardian*, at the Company's Wigan offices where Mr. Beloe reported on the progress to date: *The work on the Moss* (Glazebrook) i*s progressing favourably and the principle outlet drain is now completed up to the railway, this will enable the excavation to be carried out to the full depth required. The brickwork for the bridges over the London & North Western Railway at Kenyon, and over the Leeds-Liverpool Canal at Plank Lane are progressing favourably and the iron work is being fixed on the Houghton Cote bridge* (Slag Lane) *and that for the canal bridge is on the ground. A portion of the permanent way has been laid and the contractors have four engines* (2 stationery and 2 locomotives) *at work.*

Difficulty in meeting the increasing costs of construction led the Wigan Company to approach the Manchester, Sheffield & Lincolnshire Railway for financial assistance and the latter was allowed to subscribe to the former's dilemma by the Wigan Junction Railways Act of 17th June 1878. The same Act also authorised further deviations to the Plank Lane - Westleigh Branch, Railway E of the 1875 Act. This would now terminate further north at Pickley Green and its junction with Railway No.1 of the 1874 Act moved closer to the canal.

It had been agreed in 1875 that the Manchester, Sheffield & Lincolnshire, and Midland Railways were each to subscribe 25% of the working capital and to work services over the route for 50% of the gross receipts. Nathaniel Eckersley now took a £10,000 share interest in the Wigan Junction Railways; James Burrows had £5,000 invested, as did Thomas Stone, and the Abram Coal Company.

However, on withdrawal of the Midland Railway from the scheme in 1877, The Manchester, Sheffield & Lincolnshire Railway had promised the Wigan Directors increased support, as a safeguard against the line falling into the hands of the London & North Western Railway. Watkin had agreed to support the route financially, guaranteeing to the Wigan Company a net minimum profit of £7,500 per annum, ratified in July 1877.

Towards the end of 1878 when the 9½ mile line was 'almost' complete, the cost had increased to £176, 110. When Strangeways, Hindley, was reached, the cost had risen to £240, 426 and the contractors owed a great deal of money by the Wigan Junction Company. It is a moot question whether the Company could not, or would not pay.

In July of 1879, Richard Withers and Sir Edward Watkin of the Manchester, Sheffield & Lincolnshire Railway joined the Wigan Junction Railway Board, replacing John Stone and Samuel Thompson.

It was reported in the half-year meeting of July 1879 that the completion of the railway had been delayed by the severity of the 1878/9 winter *but it was expected that the greater portion of the line will be ready for the conveyance of traffic during the present month.* So said the *Manchester Guradian* on 27th inst.

However, as regards the opening of the route, an impasse had been reached and Watkin intervened to sort the contractors out. The latter's reply was to lift sections of track to thwart opening of the line, possibly illegal, but possession as often said, is nine-tenths of the law and Sir Edward had to climb down off his horse!

After three months of arguing and negotiation the company paid £20,000 to Thomas & Robert Stone who then re-laid the missing sections of track allowing opening of the line from Glazebrook West Junction to Strangeways Hall Colliery to take place on 16th October 1879 when an engine and three 1st Class coaches left from Stoney Lane (now Liverpool Road) Bridge, Hindley, conveying the directors and officials to Glazebrook. More officials joined the train at Glazebrook from where the party proceeded to Lowton Common to be entertained at the residence of the contractor, Robert Stone.

On reporting this occasion *The Leigh Chronicle* of 25th October 1879 quotes the Chairman of the Wigan Junction Railway, Nathaniel Eckersley, congratulating the contractors T&R Stone: *upon the excellent and thorough manner in which the contract had been carried out.* No mention of the aggravation at Strangeways, all had been forgiven. Mea culpa!

Initially, opened only to goods and mineral traffic, it would be another five years before passenger services began. It is believed the branch to the Ackers - Whitley collieries at Plank Lane opened on the same date and this short

Railway No.1 1881
Act as amended

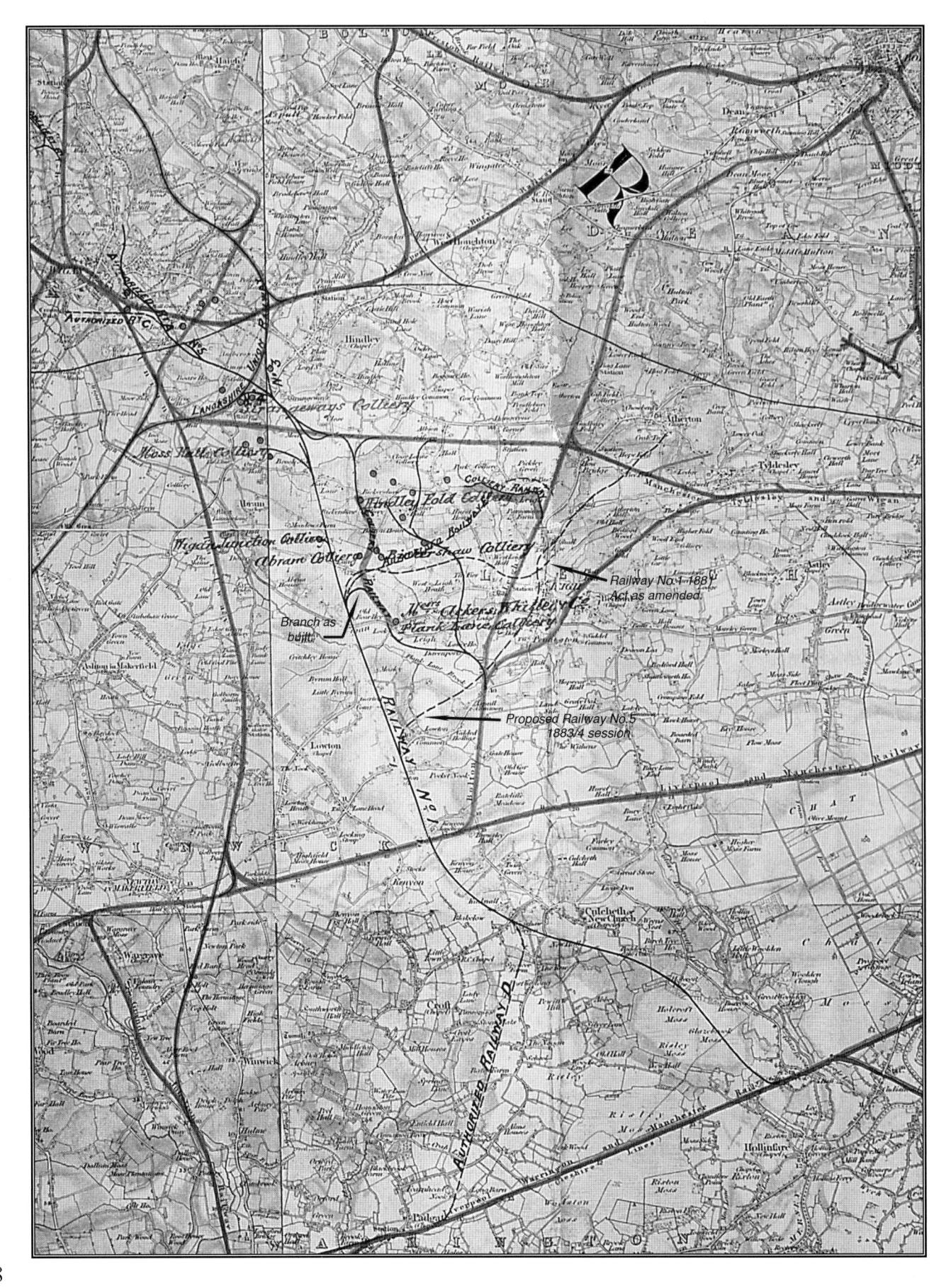

Branch as built

Proposed Railway No.5
1883/4 session

branch was the only one of a number of proposals for lines to the Westleigh Coalfield, and to Atherton, ever to be built!

The half-year meeting of the Wigan Junction Railways' shareholders of 30th January 1880, was held at the boardroom of the Manchester, Sheffield & Lincolnshire offices at London Road Station, Manchester, where Mr. Ross, the Secretary, reported that: *the local traffic between Glazebrook and the Lancashire Union Railway* had been worked by Manchester, Sheffield & Lincolnshire engines and the connection with the Lancashire Union near Strangeways Colliery had been opened for traffic since the half-year closed.* He continues; *with the consent of the Directors* (of the Company) *authorisation for the works between the Lancashire Union Railway and the Springs Branch had been given and were to proceed.* The latter is a topographical reference to the short spur at Ince which was a part of the original 1874 Act and amended in the 1875 Act following the deletion of Railway No.1 from Ince to Queen Street in its original form. See *Fig 34*.

Since the previous half-year report the Manchester, Sheffield & Linclonshire had contributed a further £20,000 (probably the same £20,000 paid to the contractors) making their total now £130,000 and a few of the principal shareholders had taken up further capital to the amount of £12,500, thus enabling the directors to complete the issue of the authorised capital under the 1874 Act and therefore able to bring into operation the borrowing powers authorised therein.

The directors of the Wigan Junction Railways were of the opinion that the line could could not be made remunerative until carried forward into Wigan and thus negotiated with their Manchester, Sheffield & Lincolnshire counterparts to the purpose of obtaining further capital to the tune of £150,000. The latter replied that any capital beyond that already advanced should be entitled to a moderate preference dividend. The Wigan Company intimated that they were prepared to accept arrangements on this basis.

Mr. Ross continues that the;- *revenue account for the period 16th October 1879 to 30th June 1880 showed total receipts of £1,289/3/-, of which 50%, £644/11/6d, was the proportion belonging to the Company and the rent charges and interest on land purchases etc would absorb the greater proportion of this amount and therefore the company were not prepared to pay any dividend on share capital since the opening of the line.*

On further reporting of the official opening of the route *The Leigh Chronicle* remarks that the 3 mile extension to Standishgate had yet to be constructed and: *the Company is waiting for more prosperous times before supplying this much needed link. Meanwhile the question of a **joint** Central Station is occupying attention and no time should be lost in supplying this want.* Strange language indeed that the mention of a joint station is raised on this occasion when previously every effort had been made to prevent such a liaison with the already established operating railway companies at Wigan!

It appears that some delay had prevented the opening of the spurs to Amberswood East & West Junctions on the Lancashire Union line, contrary to the report given by Mr. Ross on 30th January 1880. In the event, an extension of time had been granted up to 16th July 1881 for completion of the spur to Amberswood West Junction by Section 36 of the Manchester, Sheffield & Lincolnshire Railway Act of 1879. The west curve is believed to have opened in late 1882 but the east facing curve was not opened until October 1886.

* *This is a general reference to the area and not any physical connection to the Lancashire Union.*

Fig 2, left. This map of the Wigan Junction Railways proposals, and those of the Manchester, Sheffield & Lincolnshie Railway are all overdrawn on a copy of the first series Ordnance Survey completed between 1845 and 1849, no updating of the topography, apart from railways, has been added and it was a very different story by the time the Wigan Junction Railways' proposals were first mooted in 1873. Railway No.1 is the main line of the 1874 Act, and the spur, Railway No.2, (not numbered here) is the Bickershaw Branch, a short 180 degree curve. This is the only one of numerous extensions, alterations and new proposals for railways on the east side of Railway No1 in the area to be built, more details of which will be given at the appropriate location within. Railways 3&4 to the Lancashire Union Railway at Amberswood, and Railway No.5, the short spur to the Springs Branch are also of the 1874 Act. The extension to a resited station at Standishgate, Wigan, Railway A, is of the 1875 Act, as is the branch to Parson's Meadow, Railway C. The branch from Wigshaw Lane to Padgate, Railway D, is also of the 1875 Act. Railway E is of the 1875 Act but is shown here as amended by the 1878 Act. Railway B of the same Act, a branch from Railway A to the Wigan Coal & Iron Co's railway north of Rylands Sidings, also of the 1875 Act, was not allowed. It is not shown here. What confuses the issue is when was this map actually drawn? The inclusion of the London & North Western's Hindley Junctions Railway, authorised in 1883, was not completed until 1886, and the Lancashire & Yorkshire's Brindle Heath - Crow Nest Junction and Pemberton Loop lines, were not completed until 1888/9. Further, the inclusion of the Ackers-Whitley Collieries Branch, purchased in 1881 by the London & North Western, and the extensions of it to Bickershaw and Pennington Junctions were not completed until 1885. By the latter dates, many of these proposed Wigan Junction lines had been abandoned! Some notations have been added.

Courtesy, John Ryan.

Under Section 37 of the 1879 Act, the London & North Western Railway were granted running powers from Amberswood west to Strangeways Hall Colliery.

The half-yearly meeting of the Wigan Junction Railways, held at the London Road offices was chaired by Nathaniel Eckersley on 2nd February 1881, recording that: *works on the connection to the Springs Branch were proceeding but not yet complete. The ongoing negotiations with the Manchester, Sheffield & Lincolnshire Company, having for their object the provision of the necessary funds for paying off the existing liabilities of the Company, and ensuring the completion of the railway up to the town of Wigan, have resulted in an agreement between the two companies and application is being made to Parliament for powers to carry the same into effect.*

It transpired that the Manchester, Sheffield & Lincolnshire were to find a further £200,000 at $3^{1}/_{2}$% which would enable the completion of the route into Wigan. *When that has been accomplished* Mr. Eckersley comments, he hoped *they would be able to make some return to the shareholders.* When asked for a completion date by one of the latter, Mr. Eckersley replied; *a year.*

The Manchester, Sheffield & Lincolnshire Railway's New Works, Act of 18th July 1881 authorised the company to raise the additional £200,000 for the 1mile 68 chain extension to a resited station at Darlington Street from Strangeways, work beginning in the Autumn of 1881.The planned extension for a station at Standishgate, Railway 'A', of the 1875 Act, was abandoned north of Darlington Street.

Amendments had to be made to accommodate objections by the London & North Western, including the deletion of a connection from the uncompleted Amberswood East curve to the Wigan Coal & Iron Company's railway north of the Lancashire & Yorkshire's Railway at Hindley, Railway No.2 of the Act, which would have passed under the latter's railway near to their No.2 Junction. A proposal for two spurs to the Lancashire & Yorkshire Railway at Lower Ince were not allowed. See *Fig 32*. Yet further alterations to the Westleigh Branch were authorised.

A new branch from Plank Lane, Railway No.1 of the Act, was proposed to begin at $10^{1}/_{2}$ chains north of the canal bridge, almost the same point as the now existing branch to the Ackers-Whitley mines. It would run in an easterly direction before turning north to terminate on the eastern side of the Wigan Coal & Iron Company's mines at Westleigh at a point 1 furlong 6 chains north of where the London & North Western's Bolton-Kenyon line crossed the Westleigh-Atherton boundary.

At this juncture, the branch from Wigshaw Lane to Padgate on the Cheshire lines route, Railway 'D' of the 1875 Act, was abandoned.

Under the 1881 Act, the Wigan Junction Railways asked to be released from any penalties, liabilities and obligations in respect of the above abandoned proposals and, says the *Manchester Guardian* of November 26th 1880: *To provide for the payment out of court of the stocks and monies now in the Chancery Division of the High Court of Justice as security for the completion of the last mentioned railways and portion of railway.* i.e. those railways authorised by the 1881 Act.

The Westleigh Branch in particular had received short shrift from the London & North Western percolating, as it did, into an area already well catered for and the proposal went to arbitration. The planned termination of Railway No.1 of the 1881 Act on the east side the Wigan Coal & Iron Company's mines at Westleigh was deleted but an extension inserted to Chanter's Colliery at Atherton which was approved, a total line distance of 3 miles 3 furlongs.

The contract for the 1881 works was again awarded to Thomas & Robert Stone. However, work on the temporary terminus at Darlington Street, and the other stations along the route, did not begin until early 1883 because of the extensive engineering works required to cut through this built up area already saturated with roads, railways, industry and canals. Further extensions of time had been obtained under the Manchester, Sheffield & Lincolnshire and Cheshire Lines Act of 1882 and a completion date for Darlington Street Station, set no later than 16th August 1885.

The branch to Parson's Meadow (to make a connection with Winstanley Collieries Wigan Pier branch) was never built, although the land for it was purchased, and the planned incursions further into London & North Western territory in the shape of the Westleigh Branch were also dropped, for now!

By June 1883, all the track had been laid and the termini erected, and with the initiation of passenger services in mind, the completed line of railway from Glazebrook to Darlington Street was inspected by Major General Hutchinson, R.E. on behalf of the Board of Trade in February 1884. Accompanying the Inspector were Mr. Charles Sacre, Engineer-in-Chief of the Manchester, Sheffield & Lincolnshire Railway, with Mr. Bradley, Superintendent of the Company; Mr Charles H.Beloe, the Engineer of the Wigan Junction Railways, along with Mr. Hamilton, the Traffic Manager and Mr Scatcherd, Superintendent of the Signalling Department.

The Contractor, Mr. Stone, was accompanied by Mr. Lambert, his Agent, and Mr Symons, the Resident Engineer. Also in the party was Mr. Edwards of the Railway Signalling Company.

Major Hutchinson is said to have made a very careful inspection of the bridges which were tested by four of the heaviest goods locomotives and contemporary sources indicated he was *'thoroughly satisfied'*. However, according to *The Manchester Guardian* of March 24th, he had requested *a number of alterations in minor details.*

In reporting this event, the *Leigh Chronicle* quotes: *It is expected the line will be open for passenger and goods traffic throughout on March 1st*. In the event the line did not open for services between Glazebrook and Darlington Street until April 1st., after the minor details had been attended to. So obviously the Inspector was not so satisfied after all!

Under the Manchester, Sheffield & Lincolnshire Railways (Additional Powers) Act of 2nd August 1883, the extension of the Wigan Junction Railways from Darlington Street via Wigan Central to the West Lancashire Railway at New Longton was authorised, and by this route, at a cost in excess of £1½ million the Manchester, Sheffield & Lincolnshire hoped to gain access to Preston, Southport and the Fylde Coast.

It had been intended to continue the line from Wigan Central northwards to Rectory Lane at Standish, a distance of approximately 3¾ miles, crossing over the North Union near Rylands Sidings, where a short connection to the Wigan Coal & Iron Company's railway would be made, an intention that was never to come to fruition. In the event, only the 39 chain extension into Wigan ever materialised. In fact, it was not until 1887 that the land required for this short stretch was acquired, as the company were in no hurry to begin work.

In the session of 1883/4, the last and final proposal for a railway through the Westleigh Coalfield, Railway No.5, was proposed by the Manchester, Sheffield & Lincolnshire Railway. However, instead of beginning at Plank Lane, as all the earlier proposals had done, this time it would begin at Lowton St. Mary's, 74 yards north of the bridge on Newton Road Lowton, terminating again in the Atherton Township near to Chanters Colliery in a field owned by Lord Lilford. The stumbling point of this, and the previous proposed Railway No1. of the 1881 Act, is that they both percolated into an area of Westleigh that was undergoing rapid expansion, new house building in particular, and the Local Boards of Leigh and Atherton, although at first supportive of the plans gradually withdrew their consent and the proposal was withdrawn at the Committee stage.

In the half-year to 30th June 1885 the total amount of revenue was £4,315/16/10d and after deduction of working expenses etc, the deficit balance had been reduced from £2,063/12/- to £391/5/3d. Total number of passengers carried was: first class, 560; second class, 1,475 and third class, 74,431.

In the next couple of years, as per the half-yearly report of February 22nd 1888, not much improvement was made as: *the revenue account showed a credit balance of £2,194. There was, however, an increase in the amount to be provided for interest on mortgages of £764, as compared with the corresponding period last year, in consequence of the additional amount raised by loans to meet the increased capital expenditure since that date and the balance to debit of revenue account to be carried forward to the next half-year now stood at £1,799.*

By the report of February 1889, the deficit balance had increased to £2,261/7/8d. The railway was now in its tenth year of operation and still no return had been made to the shareholders.

As to the building of the railway onward from Darlington Street to Wigan Central, intense pressure was being applied by the Town Council which eventually forced the Company to proceed with the work which included diverting the River Douglas. The main contract for construction was awarded to Charles Braddock on 30th November 1889 for £28,031; Harry Rankin secured the contract for bridge and ironwork at £13,500 and Robert Neill got the contract to construct Wigan Central Station at £11,458. The extension would begin 9 chains south of Darlington Street, the lines running between the temporary station and goods sidings.

The Manchester, Sheffield & Lincolnshire Railway had paid for all extension work from Strangeways to Darlington Street, a total to June 1889 of £581,579; plus the short extension into Wigan. With a controlling interest in the line they increased their board strength to three with the appointment of J.W.McClure. R.Withers had died in 1884 and had been replaced by Edward Chapman.

There was some good news on the horizon, as in 1891 a profit was made. *Half-year receipts to June 30th came to £10,376/11/9d against £8,930/9/2d in the corresponding period in 1890, and the expenditure to £5,765/12/6d, as compared with £5,052/12/8d. The net result, after the payment of interest on mortgages and bankers interest, is a balance to the credit of revenue of £2,114/8/8d which enables the payment in full of the interest on the 5% preference shares and leaves a balance of £1,489/8/8d to be carried forward.* So reported the *Manchester Guardian* on 6th August 1891.

Passenger services over the completed route from Glazebrook to Wigan Central began on 3rd October 1892. The first station was at Culcheth, where a goods yard and sidings were built at 3½ miles from Glazebrook.

At a further 2 miles was Lowton St. Mary's Station which had a more commodious goods yard and sidings, serving the districts of Lowton Common and Golborne.

At almost 7 miles, Plank Lane Station was reached. Here were goods facilities, and connections to the Ackers-Whitley mines at Bickershaw and, later, to the Abram Coal Co's. mines. Plank Lane became Westleigh & Bedford on 1st January 1894. North of Plank Lane was Park Lane crossing and connections to Wigan Junction Colliery. The area would see more mining activity with the sinking of Maypole Colliery in the late 1890s and the provision of a halt for miners' trains from Wigan.

Bickershaw & Abram Station was adjacent to Bickershaw Lane which it would cross by a gated level crossing. Sited at 8¾ miles from Glazebrook, only very basic passenger accommodation was provided.

North of Bickershaw & Abram, on the west side of the railway, were the collieries of the Moss Hall Coal Company on the Low Hall Estate. These had been operative from the 1850s. By the time the Wigan Junction Railways arrived on the scene the collieries had been expanded and were the Moss Hall Co's. most productive pits. Further connections would be made here in the 1880s, including those with the London & North Western Railway.

After passing under the London & North Western's Springs Branch Junction - Eccles Junction lines the railway approached Strangeways & Hindley Station at 9½ miles. It would be renamed Hindley & Platt Bridge on 1st January 1892, becoming Hindley South on 1st July 1950 to distinguish it from the Lancashire & Yorkshire's Hindley North and the London & North Western's Hindley Green.

Just north of Strangeways & Hindley was Stoney Lane Bridge, later to become the A58, Liverpool Road. It was from here that the Directors Special would depart for Glazebrook on 16th October 1879 when the line opened as far as Strangeways Hall, then the extent of the line. Here connections had been made with the similarly named colliery which had been open many years previously. Having had a number of owners in the intervening years the mines were now in the possession of Crompton & Shawcross.

Passing under the Lancashire Union lines at Amberswood, Lower Ince Station was reached at 10¾ miles, just beyond which, and on the western side of the running lines, was Lower Ince engine shed, nestling in a plot of land bounded by the Lancashire & Yorkshire's line to Wigan Wallgate which passed over the Wigan Junction's lines, and Warrington Road. The railway now continued a short distance through Darlington Street which had become a goods station, to Wigan Central at 11½ miles.

As the first passenger services did not begin until 1884 there were no signal boxes in operation along the line before then with the possible exception of Lowton where, it is believed, a small cabin was installed alongside the Down, Wigan line, for controlling access to Lowton Goods Yard.

The L.N.E.R. list of 1926 gives year of manufacture only, as 1884, but this may mean 'opening date' otherwise it would have taken only three months to order, construct and install boxes at all of the following locations:- Culcheth, Bickershaw Junction, Plank Lane Sidings, Park Lane, Bickershaw & Abram, Strangeways West, Lower Ince and Wigan Goods, all being of Railway Signalling Company manufacture and, at Strangeways East, a Stevens & Company. signal box, the only one of its kind on the route. This was undoubtedly to control traffic on/off the London & North Western's Hindley Junctions lines which had opened in October 1886, and probably installed by them. Also, in the early years of operations there were some alterations to those boxes opened in 1884. Details will be given within.

However, it is known that miners' trains operated using the Moss Hall Collieries railway from the Springs Branch to Low Hall, and possibly over a part of the main line to Wigan Junction Colliery which had opened in 1880.

Glazebrook Moss Junction Cabin was a Great Central type, having been ordered in 1898. Wigan Central box was a Manchester, Sheffield & Lincolnshire type, opening concomitantly with the station.

In the half-yearly report for the period to June 1896 the Chairman, Edward Chapman, said *it was the most favourable one he remembered*. Total receipts for the past half-year were £11,899/7/9d, compared with the corresponding period for 1895 of £10,678/15/5d. The expenditure had been £6,768/3/5d as against £6,105/8/11d. *After the payment of interest on mortgages etc., the net revenue was £1,785/0/4d., which enabled the payment in full of interest on the Company's 5% preference shares, and interest at the rate of 1⅛% per annum on the 3¾% preference shares*. Nothing yet though for the ordinary shareholders!

The outlook was certainly improving and with the opening of the branch to St. Helens on 1st July the previous year, albeit for freight traffic only, it was now anticipated that the improvement of trade would continue and the days of penury were coming to an end.

As to the Wigan- New Longton line, delegations from the Fylde Coast met with the Manchester, Sheffield & Lincolnshire Board, the latter giving their wholehearted support for an extension from New Longton into Blackpool. Even a joint line with the Lancashire & Yorkshire was proposed, rejected out of hand by the latter, content that they had the upper hand! Therefore the promoters of the Blackpool Railway duly deposited their Bill which received Royal Assent at its second attempt in 1884.

From New Longton, the line would have passed through Preston, and by way of Lytham, reached Blackpool, with a short extension to Bispham at a cost in excess of £500,000. A leading light in all of these proposal was none other than Nathaniel Eckersley, Chairman of the Wigan Junction Railway, who also became Chairman of the Blackpool Company.

No work had taken place on the Wigan - New Longton route and also, despite an extension of time allowed for the Blackpool route, and an additional £100,000 contribution from the Manchester, Sheffield & Lincolnshire towards the cost of surveyors and lawyers, no progress was made on actually laying a single yard of track. Powers for construction were allowed to lapse and eventually, in 1896, after years of deliberation the New Longton - Blackpool scheme was also abandoned. According to George Dow in quoting the Board minutes of 31st July 1895, £302,000 had been spent on these two schemes and not even a cut sod to show for it!

At the half-year meeting of the Wigan Junction shareholders in February 1900, total receipts were at £15, 890 as against £16,388 for the corresonding period in 1899, with an expenditure of £8,786 against £9,044. After meeting interest charges and expenses, the net revenue was £3,615. The increase in receipts from passengers was £875; against which they had incurred a loss of £1,373 on mineral traffic. During the past six months, the Chairman reported; *there had been 158,630 passengers carried as against 136,970, an increase of 21,660; there had been 17,517 tons of goods carried but a decrease of 23,241 tons in coal traffic*. It appears that coal production had increased for the corresponding period in 1899 on account of a stoppage of production in South Wales due to a miners' strike.

Plate 3. B.R Standard Class '4' No.75018, approaches Glazebrook West Junction with a Wigan Central-Manchester Central service c1962. Glazebrook Moss Junction box is seen in the distance. *John Sloane Collection. (N.Dyckhoff).*

Sufficient profit was being made by 1904 to pay a ¾% dividend on the ordinary shares, and with the opening of the branch to St. Helens for passengers in 1900, traffic had greatly increased.

In March 1904 the terms were agreed between the Great Central Railway, the name adopted by the Manchester, Sheffield & Lincolnshire Railway from 1897, and the Wigan Junction Railways for a take-over by the former. Therefore, as from 1st January 1906, the Wigan Junction Railways ceased to exist, being fully absorbed by the Great Central Railway. The same fate applied to the Liverpool, St. Helens & South Central Lancashire Railway, the name adopted by the St. Helens & Wigan Junction Railways in 1889. In 1923 all were to become a part of the London & North Eastern Railway, and finally, on 1st January 1948, British Railways.

Plate 4. If Railway D of the 1875 Wigan Junction Railways Act had gone ahead it would have made a junction with the Cheshire lines route east of Padgate Station, just beyond the signal box seen on the left. This view, which dates from the mid-1930s, is of a westbound (inward) Continental Express approaching the station at speed. Unfortunately, the 1/100 shutter speed used for this glass lantern slide was not sufficiently fast enough to stop the locomotive and it thus remains unidentified.

Author's Collection.

Plate 5. Class 'O4/8' 2-8-0 No.63721 passes through Glazebrook Station on 21st June 1957 with a westbound coal train. On the left is Dam Lane Head. The goods yard has a healthy contingent of vans in the siding.

Ben Brooksbank. Reproduced under the Creative Commons Licence.

GLAZEBROOK

Plate 6. LNER Class 'D9' 4-4-0 No.2325, in full flight, passes through Glazebrook Station with an eastbound express on 18th October 1946. Over on the left is Glazebrook Goods Yard, the subject of an agreement of 18th August 1891 between the Manchester, Sheffield & Lincolnshire Railway and the Cheshire Lines Committee. The former were allowed to use the yard for interchange traffic, paying the latter £30.00 per year and 50% of maintenence costs. The sidings were to be under the control of the Cheshire Lines who will also have free use of said sidings and take up or construct additional works as they see fit.

John Sloane Collection (H.C.Casserley).

On 1st July 1900 a new curve, Dam Lane - Glazebrook Moss Junction opened. This had been sanctioned by the Cheshire Lines Committee Act of 25th May 1900, thus enabling direct Wigan/ St. Helens - Warrington through services.

The first passenger trains to use the new curve began in 1903 when six trains ran from Wigan Central to Warrington Central and five in the opposite direction. Only one train ran directly from St. Helens to Warrington but two from Warrington to St. Helens. The object of these services was to facilitate connections to Liverpool, Widnes and Southport. It could hardly compete though with the existing services from Wigan Wallgate to Liverpool and Southport, the Lancashire & Yorkshire line being much more direct, or indeed with the London & North Western's trains from St. Helens. In the event all the passenger services using the Dam Lane - Glazebrook Moss curve were withdrawn in 1909.

For many years, race specials from Liverpool would use this curve along with the occasional Rugby League special from Warrington Central to Wigan Central. The attendant horse box specials from Newmarket and Lambourne to Haydock would use West Junction.

Glazebrook Moss Junction was officially taken out of use in May 1965 but its last day of operation was Saturday 31st October 1964, the last turn being 8.32am to 12.16pm. The Glazebrook Triangle was also used to turn locomotives which had worked into Glazebrook Sidings, prior to working their return journey. This arrangement came into operation after use of the turntable on the Up side at Glazebrook Station was abolished*.

*From information supplied by Tim Oldfield.

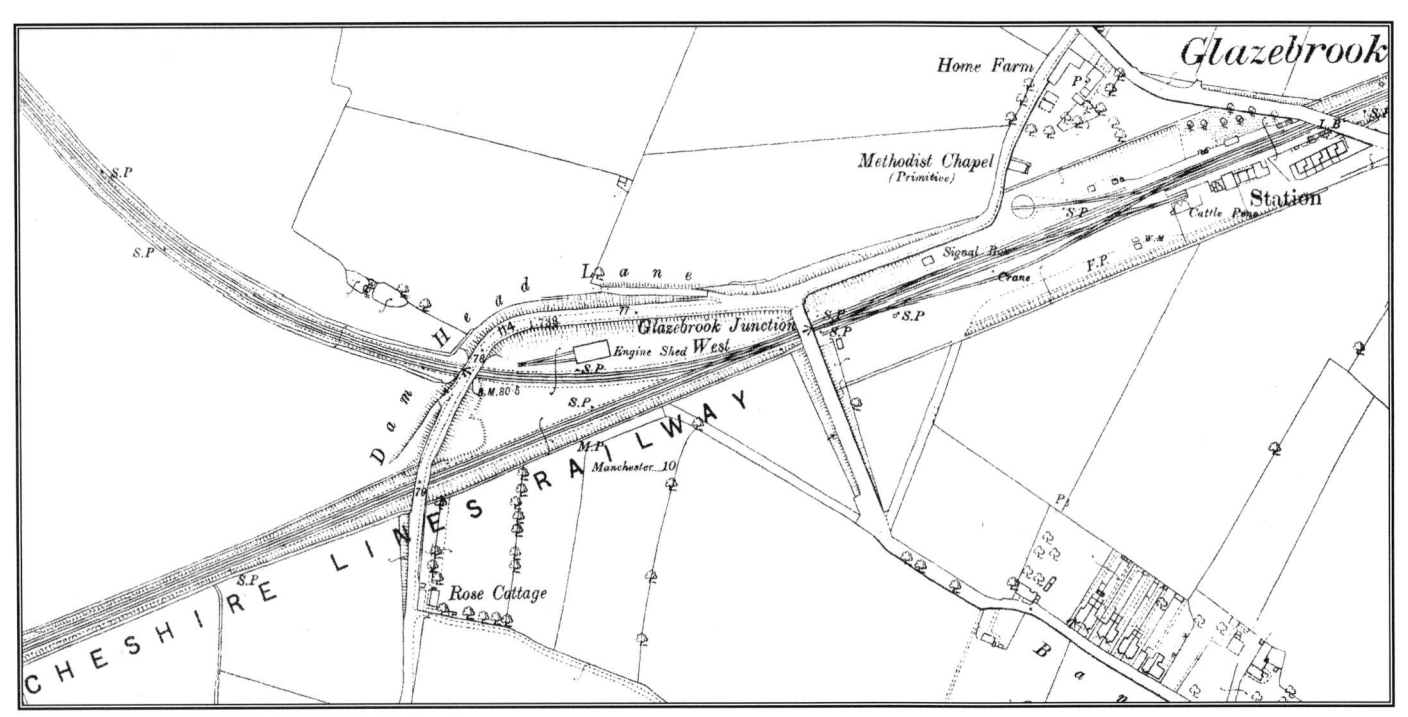

Fig 3. Glazebrook West Junction and station c1892. Strangely, an engine shed is shown near West Junction but unconnected to the running lines! Had this been for the contractors use?

Plate 7. A Manchester bound DMU approaches Dam Lane Junction on 1st August 1962. *Eddie Bellass.*

Plate 8. Glazebrook Moss Junction and signal box photographed on 26th August 1956. The view is looking south towards the curve to Dam Lane Junction on the right. The box is a Great Central Railway type '4', all timber, built on a brick base.
Signalling Record Society.

Plate 9. A two car DMU treads carefully past Dam Lane Junction on 1st August 1962. There is obviously some P.W. work in progress as the platelayer signals to the driver to proceed slowly. In the left background, between signal and telegraph pole, is the bridge over the Glazebrook Moss - Glazebrook West Junction curve.
Eddie Bellass.

Plate 10. Class '31' No.31 464 passes through Glazebrook Station on 2nd August 1986 bound for Liverpool Lime St. Even this view is no longer possible today as tree growth has taken over the embankment and former goods yard on the right. *Gerry Bent.*

Plate 11. 'Director' Class 4-4-0 No.62654 *Walter Burgh Gair* takes the Wigan route at Glazebrook West Junction with six compartment coaches on 11th August 1953 on a mid-afternoon service as a passing 'Stanier '8F' and brake van are held at West Junction home signal. 62654 was withdrawn a few days later. *Bob McClellan Collection.*

L.N.E.R.
GLAZEBROOK MOSS JC.

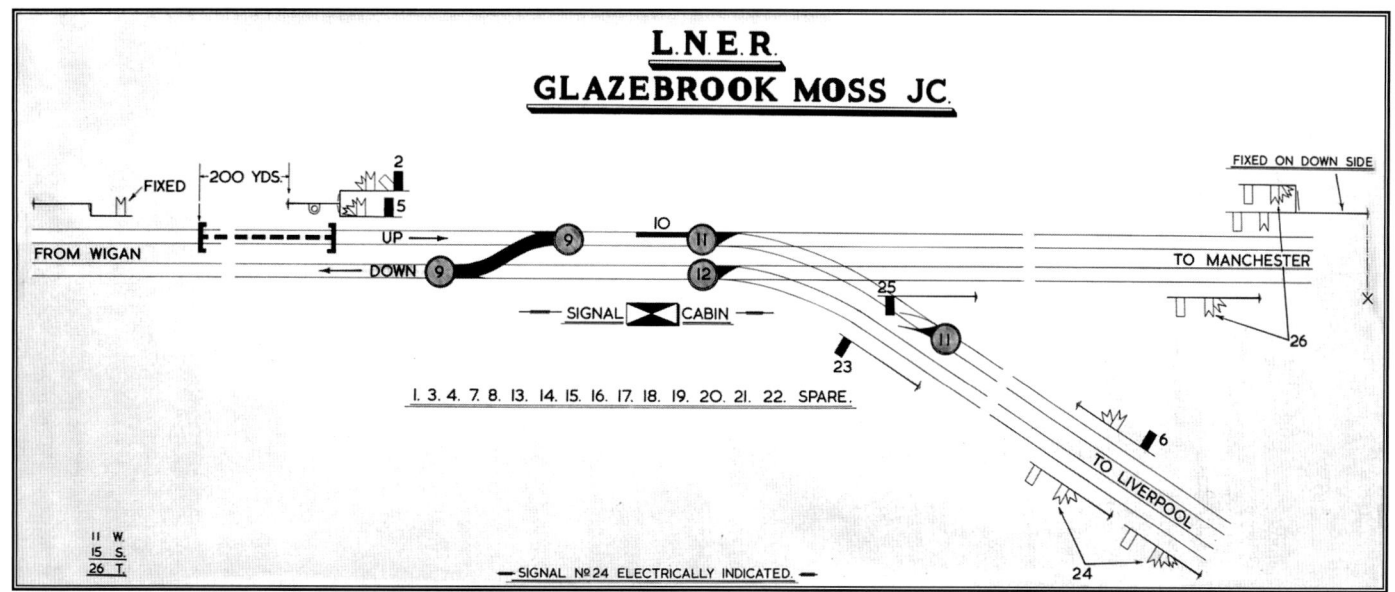

Fig 4. Glazebrook Moss Junction c1930.

Plate 12. The view northwards from Dam Lane Head towards Glazebrook Moss Junction on 11th September 2012. The trackbed from Glazebrook West Junction enters the picture at middle right, whilst the curve from Dam Lane Junction comes in at middle left. The former Glazebrook Moss Junction is just beyond the trees, middle centre. *Author.*

Plate 13. Viewed from a passing train, the curve to Glazebrook Moss Junction is seen to pass under the extant Dam Head Lane Bridge on 14th November 1964. Again though, the area is, today, colonised by tree growth. *John Ryan.*

NEWCHURCH HALT AND RISLEY ROF

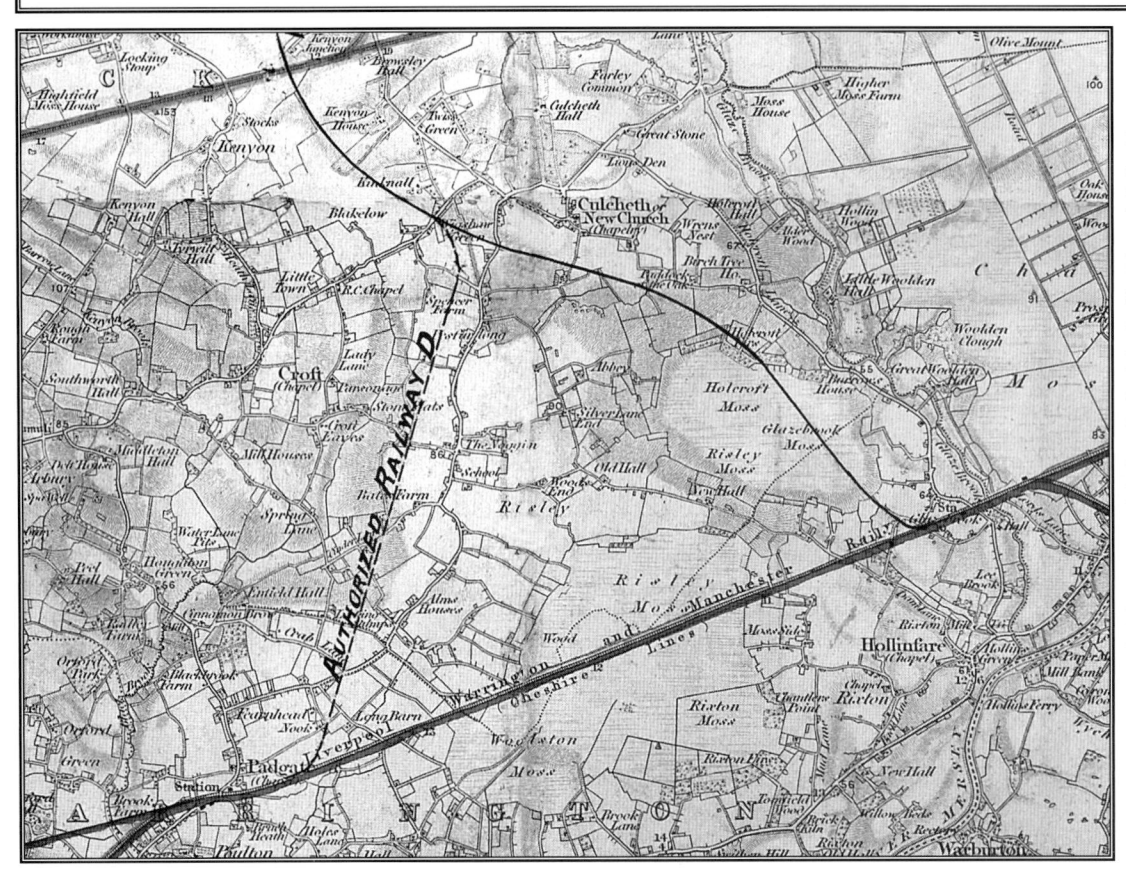

Fig 5. The branch to meet the Cheshire Lines at Padgate authorised by Railway D under the 1875 Act would have begun at Wigshaw Lane, Culcheth, cutting across the area later occupied by Risley ROF. The finances of the railway company were severely stretched and as a consequence the project was dropped in 1881.

It will be noted that the site of Culcheth Station has not yet been decided upon.

Courtesy, John Ryan.

Plate 14. A late view of Newchurch Halt as viewed towards Glazebrook. Admiralty Sidings Signal Box was sited on the right, just beyond the overbridge.
John Ryan.

The Newchurch Halt - Risley Royal Ordnance Factory (R.O.F.) Branch is believed to have opened in 1942, although it did not appear in the timetables until early 1943, and, it is thought, used for passenger services only. This seems to make sense when the layout is examined; it would have been much easier to use the C.L.C. lines for munitions purposes.

The branch from Newchurch was used to ferry munitions workers from Wigan and intermediate stations into the works. The 'Halt' itself was constructed of pre-fabricated concrete slabs resting on brick piers. Two old Great Eastern Railway coaches were provided to serve as ticket office/ waiting rooms/ stores etc, one on the up platform near the station steps and the other part way along it.

The single line into Risley R.O.F. was 1mile 46 chains in length and left the main lines just after the A574 road overbridge, controlled by a new brick and concrete signal box on the west side of the lines.

Built at Government expense, the branch ran from a point 70 chains south of Culcheth Station, to a station within the R.O.F. boundary. There were four platforms and the station had M.o.D. type brick and concrete buildings. The line had a 15mph speed limit worked by single line token obtained from Newchurch signal box.

During the war years the L.N.E.R. had two or three King's Cross suburban articulated sets transferred to the Wigan/St. Helens lines for use on the workmen's trains to Risley. These were eight coach sets made up of two 'Quads' - a brake third and three thirds - with seating for 648. It was reported that when the first of these sets ran from St. Helens the destination indicators still showed "Moorgate" and "Finsbury Park". One set was still in the area in late 1947, although not working to Risley, noted working the following services:-

5.25am (SO) Wigan to Westleigh & Bedford (ECS).
5.46am (SO) Westleigh & Bedford to Wigan.
6.10am (SO) Wigan to Irlam.
8.00am (SO) Irlam to Wigan.
6.10am (SX) Wigan to Manchester Central.
7.40am (SX Manchester Central to Wigan.
3.40pm (SX) Wigan to Irlam.
5.25pm (SX) Irlam to Wigan.

The line from Newchurch was in regular use until 7th July 1945 when the signal box was shown as closed in the W.T.T. Afterwards the box was opened as and when required, at least until 20th January 1948 for crippled wagon storage on the single track until these were required at Dewsnap. 'J10' No.5151 was a regular on these duties and 'J11s' Nos. 4298, 4311 & 4437 also made appearances, along with another 'J10' No.5208. The signal arms at Newchurch are reported as removed c1951 and the box permanently switched out. The signal box at Newchurch, also known as 'Admiralty Sidings S.B.' was demolished on 22nd April 1967.

Plate 15. Fairburn 2-6-4T No.42072 arrives at Newchurch Halt with a Manchester service. The station was provided with two old Great Eastern Railway coach bodies. The one furthest away was a waiting shelter, whilst one on the platform was used as a ticket office, store and toilet. Along with other stations along the route, it would close on 2nd November 1964. Services between Wigan Central and Risley C.L.C., down to one each way in 1960 ceased in January 1962.
John Sloane Collection.

Fig 6. Newchurch Halt and Risley Royal Ordnance c1944.

Fig 7, below. Newchurch Halt and connection to Risley ROF. *Courtesy, Tim Oldfield.*

Risley ROF was one of a number of 'filling' factories that were built in various parts of the country at the beginning of W.W.II. The site at Risley covered in excess of 920 acres. It was built on mossland often covered by low cloud or mist which it was said, was the very reason for it being built here, thus being unobservable from the air. Construction began in August 1939, taking about 18 months to complete. They were known as filling factories because the shell casings were filled with the explosive mixture before being transported to one of the storage bunkers.

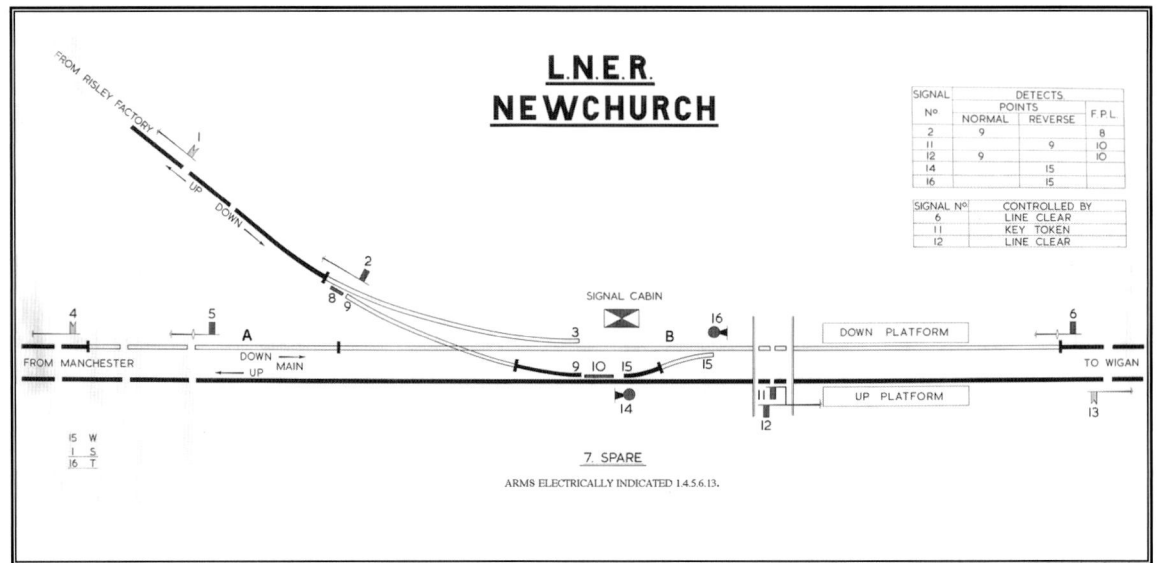

Risley was factory No.6, and in all there were about 20 such factories built, Chorley ROF being No.1. This was all part of the Government's strategy to expand the capacity of the manufacturing of armaments and ammunition, and the wider dispersal of these ROFs around the country and away from the South of England where they were more vulnerable to enemy air raids. A great deal of emphasis had to be given to safety and various precautionary features were incorporated into the site layout. Reinforced concrete blast walls; high grassed embankments concealing storage bunkers below; with generous open spaces between them.

The factory received the filling explosives in bulk by rail from other ROF installations. After the casings had been filled and stored, special munitions trains would collect a number of vans and disperse the armaments to wherever they were needed most at any particular time. More often that not, these trains ran at night.

22

CULCHETH

Plate 16. One of the Ivatt Class '2' 2-6-0s calls at Culcheth in September 1960 with a service for Wigan Central. Like the station, the small goods shed appears to be in good condition having been well maintained but by this period traffic into the yard was infrequent as only two wagons, a 10 ton open near the shed, and a box van behind the station, are in view. The goods yard was out of use in late 1964. The signal box is one of the Railway Signalling Company's installations. *Eddie Bellass*

When passenger services on the railway to Wigan began in 1884, Culcheth was the first station on the line. Originally in Lancashire, since boundary reorganisation in 1974, is now in Cheshire. The village of Culcheth is mentioned in the Doomsday Book and is therefore pre-Norman. In fact, the village features on Saxon maps of South Lancashire as 'Calchuth' or Calchyth'.

After the Norman Conquest, the de Risley, de Holcroft and de Culcheth families had residence here, each contributing to the crest of Culcheth.

The Wigan Junction Act of 1875 authorised a branch line from Wigshaw Lane at Culcheth to the Cheshire Lines route at Padgate so giving access to Warrington from Wigan and/or St. Helens but like many of the proposals put forward by various Acts, was abandoned under the the Manchester, Sheffield & Lincolnshire New Works Act of 1881. As paymasters, the latter were anxious to reduce expenditure and not disposed to fund a lengthy cut-off line of dubious merit through open country. In effect, the Glazebrook Moss Junction - Dam Lane Junction curve, which opened in 1900, did the same job for a fraction of the cost.

The area was then, principally a farming community and passenger traffic was sparse, although some freight traffic could be accommodated in the small goods yard which in fact did not close until 1965. The passenger service was withdrawn and the station closed on 2nd November 1964.

Plate 17. A footbridge (bridge 10) sited north-west of Culcheth Station began off Hob Hey Lane at Newchurch and gave access to an isolated farm. Seen beyond the footbridge is a farm occupation bridge. *Peter Hampson.*

Plate 18. A Manchester bound service with Stanier 2-6-4T No.42456 in charge calls at Culcheth also in September 1960. The same two wagons are seen in the goods yard and the same woman waits on the platform as in *Plate 16.* *Eddie Bellass.*

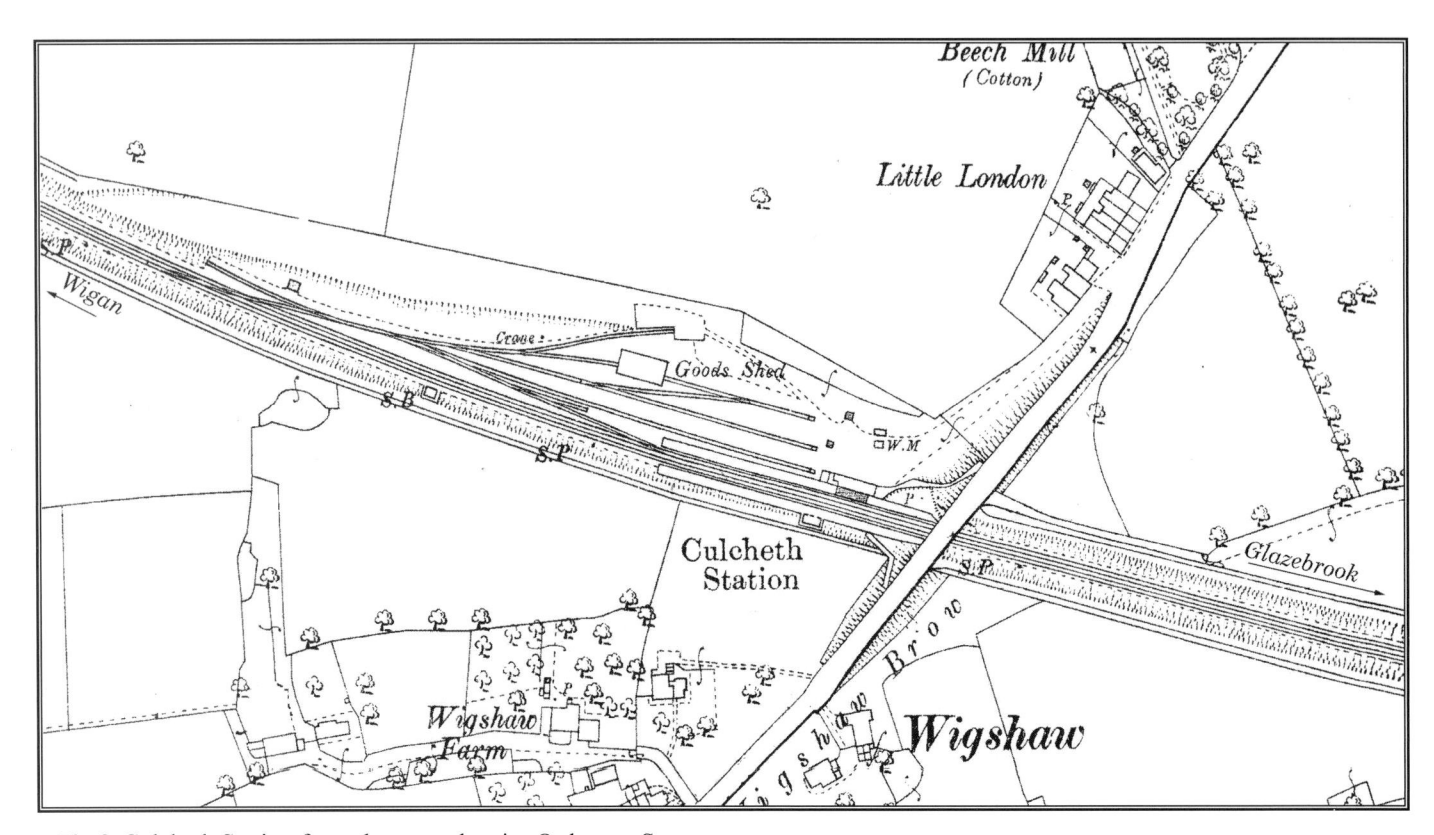

Fig 8. Culcheth Station from the second series Ordnance Survey.

Plate 19. 42456 gets away from Culcheth as a Leigh Corporation bus passes over on Wigshaw Lane above. *Eddie Bellass.*

Plate 20. Type '2' diesel No.D5277 is seen at Culcheth in July 1964 with a Wigan Central - Manchester Central train of six coaches. The goods yard sidings have been lifted leaving just a short headshunt off the up line. *Eddie Bellass.*

Plate 21. On the last day of service, 1st November 1964, B.R.Standard Class '4' No.75057 calls at Culcheth with the 2.15p.m. Irlam - Wigan Central. This is one of the workmen's trains on which the morning shift would be returning home.. *Peter Eckersley.*

Plate 22. This low level view of Culcheth Station from March 1961 shows it to be in fairly good condition and not having been subjected to the usual attacks of vandalism, often the case elsewhere. All the fencing seems to be intact and well maintained. The poster on the gable end advertises holidays in Northern Ireland, whilst the nearest poster on the platform side gives details of trips to Blackpool for 6s/9d (32 pence in today's money) - a bit steep when compared to what the motor coach firms were offering at around 2/- cheaper. *Eddie Bellass.*

Plate 23. A deserted Culcheth Station is seen in this 1964 view looking towards Glazebrook. *Tim Oldfield.*

Plate 24. A youthful Peter Hampson emerges from the waiting room on the Wigan platform at Culcheth in November 1964 after passenger services had ceased. *Tim Oldfield.*

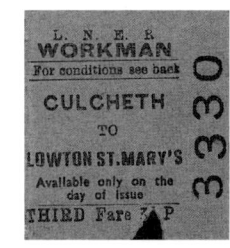

Ticket, courtesy, Tom Sherratt.

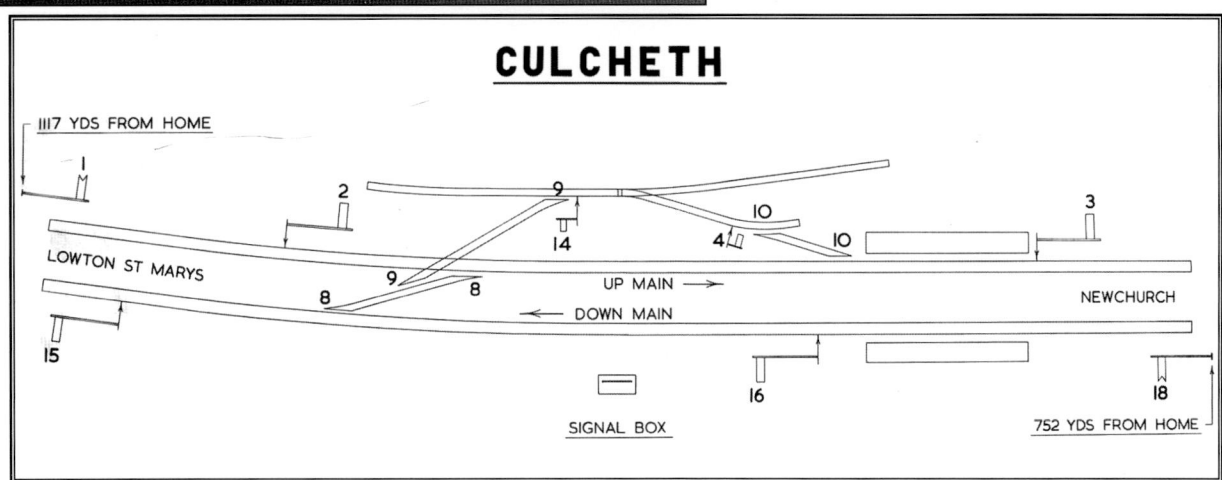

Fig 9. Culcheth Station and goods yard c1960. *Courtesy, Tim Oldfield.*

27

Plate 25. With steam to spare, a Wigan Central - Manchester Central service crosses over the Liverpool - Manchester line at Kenyon in July 1964. In January 2013, the proposed route of HS2 North was announced. If it is ever built in its present form it will pass over the Liverpool-Manchester lines here at this same location. *Eddie Bellass.*

Plate 26. An ex-L.M.S. 0-6-0 '4F' has just crossed over the Liverpool-Manchester line at Kenyon with a rake of mineral empties, possibly for Golborne Colliery c1961, and is approaching the road-over bridge on Wilton Lane. The footbridge is of the archetypal 'Hornby-Dublo' design. *Eddie Bellass.*

Plate 27. Class '2' No.46428 crosses the Liverpool & Manchester line at Kenyon c1948. These 2-6-0 engines were designed by H.G.Ivatt for the L.M.S. and first introduced in 1946. No.46428, together with No. 46434, were shedded at Lower Ince until closure.
W.D.Cooper, Cooperline.

Plate 28. Class 'J10' No. 65208, in early British Railways livery, leaves the environs of Kenyon behind and is seen on the approach to Lowton St. Mary's with a Wigan train on 3rd May 1949. At the time, Lower Ince Shed had an allocation of these engines.
W.D.Cooper, Cooperline.

Plate 29. Seen on the Liverpool-Manchester line, type '2' No.D7619 & crane have been engaged on removing the now redundant railway bridge which spanned the route as seen in *Plate 25.* This work was carried out overnight - Saturday/Sunday 13th/14th June 1970.
Gerry Bent.

Plate 30. One of the forty-strong class of Stanier 2-6-0 'Moguls' No.42970 approaches Wilton Lane at Kenyon in May 1959 with a Wigan Central - Manchester Central train. To give the reader some orientation the building in the right background is Butt's Mill at Leigh.
Eddie Bellass.

LOWTON ST. MARY'S

From 1874 onwards, a number of branch railways had been proposed for incursion into the Westleigh Coalfield from Plank Lane and all had come up against opposition from the London & North Western Railway even though some had been authorised for construction. By the early 1880s the Leigh Local Board, in their quest to persuade the London & North Western Railway to improve facilities at Leigh & Bedford Station courted both the Lancashire & Yorkshire and the Manchester, Sheffield & Lincolnshire Railways for improved facilities. They had publicly stated a preferrence for the latter.

Already flushed with their incursions into London & North Western territory, in 1884 the Manchester, Sheffield & Lincolnshire Railway proposed a branch from Lowton St. Mary's, to terminate near Chanter's Colliery at Hindsford, between Tyldesley and Atherton.

The branch would begin 74 yards north of Newton Road at Lowton running towards Pennington in a north-easterly direction where it would cross the Bolton - Kenyon line at Pennington. Then, by a more northerly route cross Church Fields and Leigh Road, Leigh, before continuing to Hindsford, passing under the London & North Western's Tyldesley-Wigan line at Chanter's Sidings, east of Howe Bridge. However, the Leigh Local Board objected to any incursion into the Church Fields area as this would prevent any housing development between the Bolton - Kenyon line and Leigh Road, which, in fact, had already begun, the first housing on Glebe Street completed about 1880.

At a meeting between the two parties, the Leigh Local Board suggested an alternative route from Plank Lane with a connection to the Wigan Coal & Iron Co's. Sovereign Pit at Westleigh and with the Fletcher - Burrows Collieries at Atherton. This was in fact, very similar to the previously authorised scheme in the Manchester, Sheffield & Lincolnshire's New Works Act of 1881 and not too far diverse from Railway E of the 1875 Act.

The Company indicated they would press on with their present scheme but were willing to incorporate clauses as regards the objections to embankments and street openings put forward by the Leigh local Board.

The London & North Western, ever mindful of these more recent events, had purchased the Ackers-Whitley private line now being converted to a through route between Pennington South Junction and Bickershaw Junction and, in March 1884, had proposed a new line from Huyton, through St. Helens, Ashton-in-Makerfield, Edge Green and

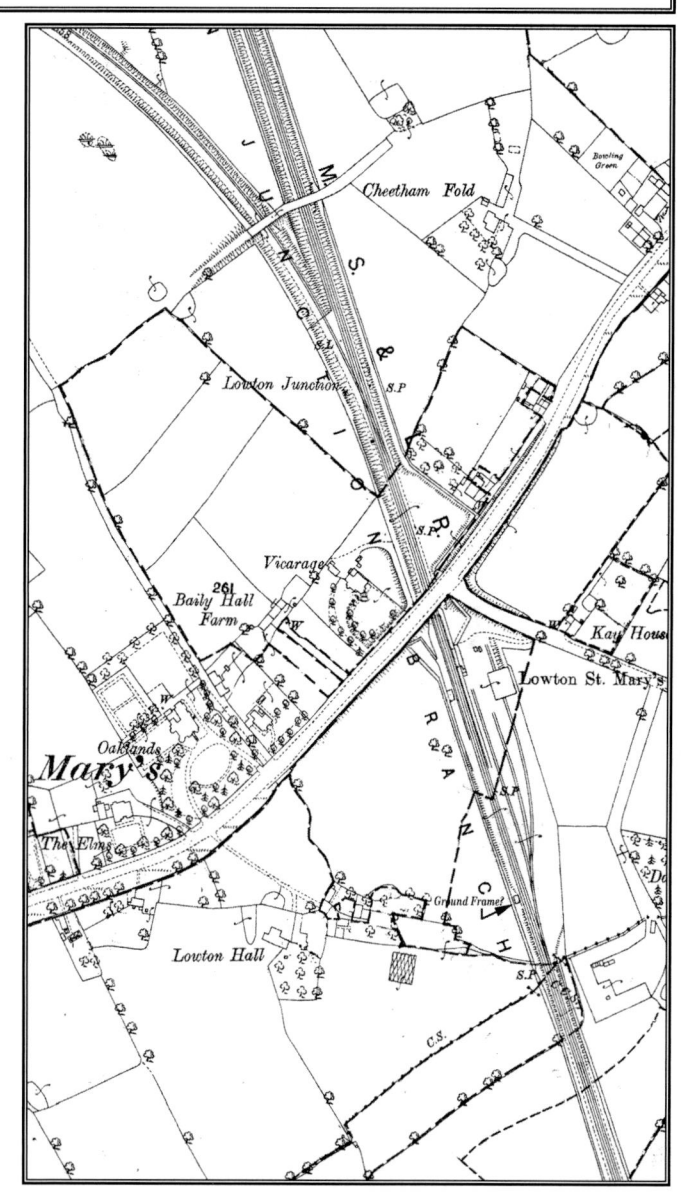

Fig 10. From the second series Ordnance Survey of 1892 the general layout of Lowton St. Mary's is seen but note at this period only a single line from St. Helens connects with the main lines here. Neither are there any exchange sidings on the St. Helens Branch for, technically, this was a junction between two independent railways and exchange sidings would later be provided.

It will be noted that no signalling installations are shown on this edition. However, there is a small cabin at the southern end of the Wigan platform which, it is believed, must have been a ground frame for controlling access and egress into Lowton Goods Yard. Also, the platforms are indistinct on this edition and it may be that some modifications were carried out before the passenger services over the St. Helens Branch began in 1900.

Leigh, a total length of approximately 9 miles. It would then follow the existing route through Tyldesley to Eccles Junction. Some comment is expressed in favour of the London & North Western's plan and the Editorial in the *Leigh Chronicle* of 16th May 1884, whose opinions generally followed the views of the Leigh Local Board, urged the North Western to construct the branch from St. Helens as quickly as possible.

In late October 1884, the Manchester, Sheffield & Lincolnshire Company's engineer, Mr. Beloe, had looked more favourably on the Leigh Board's suggestions, re the route via Sovereign Pit from Plank Lane, and had asked if they had any further comments or suggestions to make before final plans were drawn up.

In reply, the Leigh Local Board urged that the bridge over Wigan Road should not be less than 45ft wide, or if levels permit, should go under it. An arched bridge was requested to span Glebe Street and that a proposed goods station should be situated between Stock Platt and Kirkhall Lane, on the Westleigh side of Leigh Road. Mr Beloe indicated it was not possible to go under Wigan Road because of the levels required to approach the goods yard. All other conditions were agreed to by the Company and for their part, the Leigh Local Board promised to wholeheartedly support the scheme when it came before Parliament.

Having reached agreement with the Leigh Board the Manchester Sheffield & Lincolnshire now found themselves at odds with the Atherton Local Board who objected to the scheme on the grounds that there would be no station within a half-mile of Atherton town centre. The line to the Wigan Coal & Iron Company's Sovereign Pit which continued eastwards to Fletcher-Burrows Chanters Pits, carried the railway into the Atherton Township and the Atherton Board, having secured an agreement with the Lancashire & Yorkshire Railway for their planned Pendleton-Atherton-Hindley, Crow Nest Junction route, saw no advantage in having a railway terminating within their boundaries yet providing no passenger facilities for them. It is difficult to know where the Atherton Board got the idea that this was anything other than a mineral line as

Plate 31. This photo at Lowton St. Mary's of Great Central Class '12AM' 2-4-0T No.448 dates from about 1910, after the passenger service to St. Helens Central had begun, as seen from the station sign. These engines were built by Sacre for the Manchester South Junction & Altrincham line in 1880/1 as Class '12AT'. As the length of trains over that route increased these small engines found the additional weight difficult to cope with. Three engines, Nos.23, 24 & 448, were fitted with push-pull apparatus in 1906, three more being converted a while later and all redesignated as Class '12AM'. *Author's Collection.*

Plate 32. A very early view of Lowton St. Mary's Station looking north towards Newton Road bridge beyond which is the junction for St. Helens opposite the signal box. The sign says 'change here for Golborne, Ashton - in - Makerfield, Haydock and St. Helens'. However, this was not always the case as at various periods the through trains ran from St. Helens necessitating a change for Wigan passengers.
Author's Collection.

there is no mention in any of the previous proposals by the Manchester, Sheffield & Lincolnshire of passenger facilities. It can only be assumed that it was a ploy to favour the Lancashire & Yorkshire route which was to open in 1888.

However, continued pressure for further changes from the Leigh group led to the withdrawal of the plan before it reached Committee Stage and the Leigh Local Board congratulated themselves on successfully thwarting the plan.

Neither the London & North Western's line from St. Helens to Leigh, or the Manchester, Sheffield & Lincolnshire's line from Plank Lane to Atherton were ever built.

Initially, there were seven trains each way per day when passenger services began from Darlington Street on 1st April 1884. Departures from Darlington Street were timed at:- 8.40am, 11.15am, 12.00 noon, 1.45pm, 5.05pm, 7.00pm & 8.00pm. Return Workings left Manchester Central at:- 10.05am, 10.40am, 12.35pm, 3.20pm, 5.45pm, 6.45pm, & 8.15pm. Of these, two were express trains, the 10.40am from Manchester stopping only at Glazebrook and arriving at Darlington Street at 11.15am. The return at 12 noon to Manchester ran non-stop in 30 minutes. However, the express trains lasted only until late 1887 but seven trains still worked each way Monday - Friday with an extra train on Saturdays. On Sundays, two trains left Darlington Street at 9.30am & 8.00pm with return workings at 8.05am & 6.45pm.

When the line to St. Helens from Lowton opened for regular passenger services on 3rd January 1900, six trains ran each way Monday - Saturday and of these, five ran non-stop in both directions between St. Helens and Manchester Central the odd one out working only to Lowton. On Sundays three trains ran, two of these again working non-stop.

By July 1900 the number of trains had been increased to ten trains each way between St. Helens and Manchester Central, passengers for Wigan having to change at Lowton. Sunday workings were four between St. Helens and Glazebrook, Wigan passengers having to change twice!

An about turn occurred in 1903 when the services from Manchester ran through to Wigan, a shuttle service operating from Lowton to St. Helens Central. Again on Sundays the trains terminated at Glazebrook necessitating two changes for St. Helens passengers. There were two additional trains which ran only between Wigan and Lowton St Mary's.

In 1910, eight trains ran between Wigan Central and Manchester Central with an extra two on Saturdays between Wigan and Culcheth, St. Helens passengers still having to change at Lowton. Around 1914 the service pattern was reversed with direct St. Helens - Manchester trains connecting with services from Wigan at Lowton. The two additional trains between Wigan and Lowton still ran with a further two between Wigan and Culcheth on Fridays and Saturdays plus a late evening train from Wigan to Irlam connecting with Manchester services on the Cheshire Lines route. Sundays was limited to three trains each way from St. Helens to Manchester.

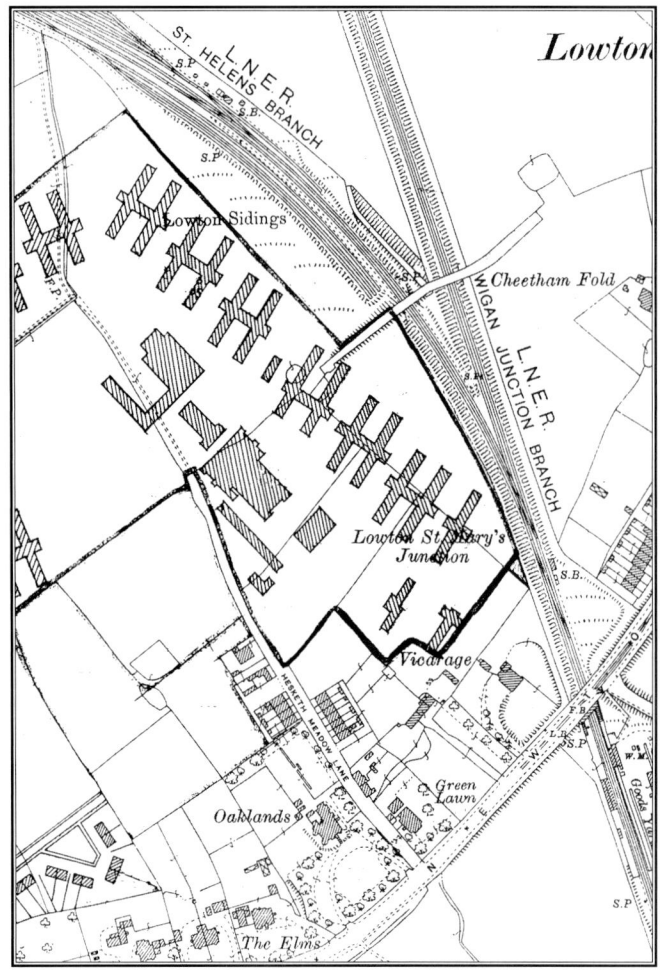

Fig 11. The completed double-track arrangement for the St. Helens branch at Lowton St. Mary's Junction is shown on this updated, post-war Ordnance Survey.

The two Lowton Signal boxes shown are namely:- Lowton Sidings alongside the sidings on the St. Helens Branch opened, according to the Inspecting Officer's report, on 23rd December 1899, and Lowton Junction north of Newton Road overbridge which opened in July 1895, and is probably concomitant with the opening of the St. Helens Branch to freight traffic. Previously the signalling at Lowton is believed to have been worked by the ground frame shown in *Fig 10* at the south end of the Wigan platform, opposite the goods yard.

The cabin north of Newton Road was replaced c1930 by a new Lowton St. Mary's Junction installation having a 36 lever frame which was built in the triangle of the Wigan and St. Helens lines. This new box also made the 1899 cabin on the St. Helens Branch redundant and a ground frame was installed here. Details are given in *Fig 12.*

Again, with reference to HS2 North, working off details so far available, the line is shown to pass under Newton Road on the Western side of the timber yard which today occupies the former trackbed of the Wigan Junction lines.

The 'H' blocks prominent in *Fig 11* have an interesting history. In 1939, at the beginning of W.W.II., the War Department requisitioned fields at Hesketh Meadows to be used as an accommodation village for the munitions factory at Risley Moss. It was to be known as Risley Hostels.

Construction, which was to take about 12 months, began in 1941 and was to accommodate some 600 workers. It would appear therefore, that the War Department were thinking of bringing in workers from much further afield than the local townships. The logic of building the accommodation, which had its own chapel, school and mess facilities at this location is obvious; just a short walk to Lowton St. Mary's Station to board the train and the workers would be at Risley very quickly. However, in 1942, before any workers had arrived the plans were changed and it was decided that it would become a land based Navy establishment.

The base was to be known as H.M.S. CABBALA, a wartime Royal Naval Signalling School where ratings and wrens underwent training in three separate branches of signals; wireless telegraphy, visual signalling and coding.

Every unit of the navy is, in essence, a ship and carries the prefix H.M.S., irrespective of it being a floating ship or a land based collection of buildings. H.M.S. CABBALA utilised the brick built accommodation blocks with the 'cabins' on each long side of the 'H'; the cross piece was a sitting room. There was a large hall and stage which provided for lectures, film shows, entertainment and a weekly dance. A self-contained sick bay was well staffed and a N.A.A.F.I. canteen was serviced by a battery of stewards and cooks who provided meals which, when compared to the civilian diet of the time, were said to be superb. In all, up to 600 sailors and 500 wrens were fed and watered each day.

A parade ground was a prerequisite of any military establishment and facilities for outdoor games took place on surrounding fields requisitioned by the Admiralty for this purpose. The site ceased to be used by the Navy in 1946.

In 1950, the base was reopened as 'Scotia North', providing accommodation for U.S. Servicemen and their dependents as an outpost of Burtonwood Air Base. Each of the 'H' blocks were converted into 5/8 apartments, totalling 110 units of accommodation. In some instances the internal walls were demolished to make larger rooms and all of the units were redecorated and had steam heating. Each block had its own washroom for laundry and hardstanding for vehicles.

The Americans remained until 1960 when the then Golborne U.D.C. took over the site, using the adjacent land for sports fields and taking the former accommodation into their housing stock. Opening of Lowton Civic Hall by Golborne U.D.C. took place in early 1963. When, in 1974, Golborne U.D.C. became a part of Wigan Metropolitan Borough, it was decided to demolish the housing units and replace them with new council housing nearby but to retain the playing fields.

From time to time reunions for former naval personnel who served at H.M.S. CABBALA have been held here, the last being on 22nd April 1989.

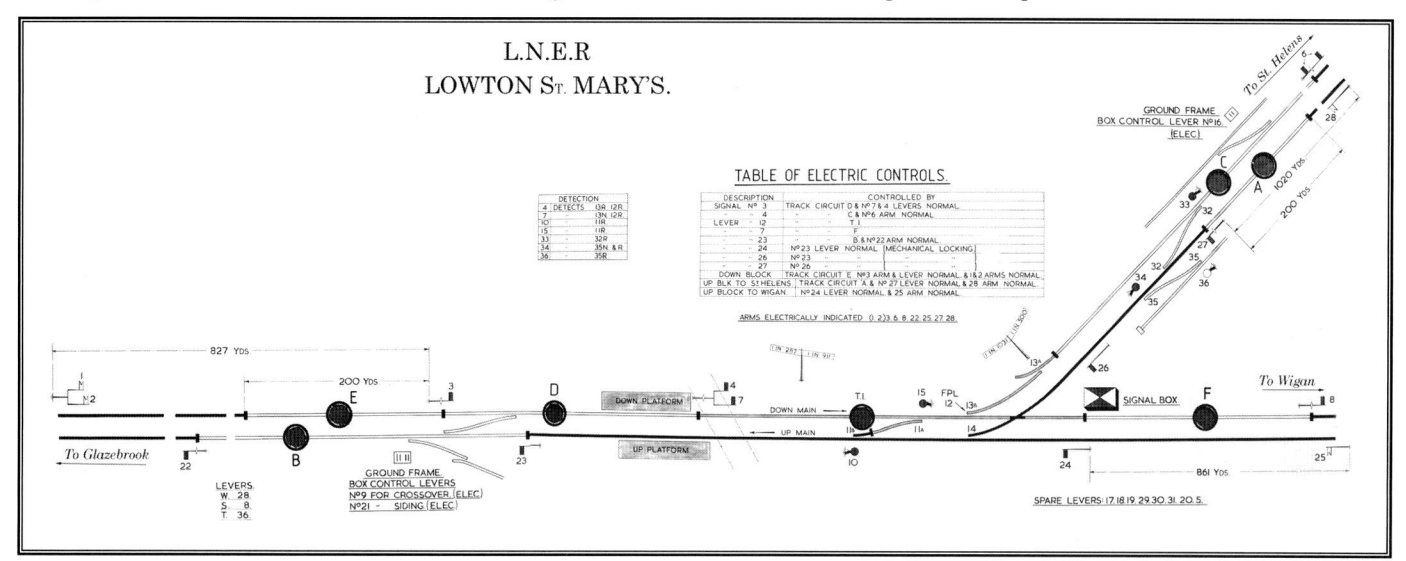

Fig 12. Details of the new Lowton St. Mary's signal box c1930s. *Courtesy, Tim Oldfield.*

Plate 33. A busy scene at Lowton St.Mary's with Fairburn 2-6-4T No.42295 in the goods siding as Stanier 2-6-4T No.42447 departs with a Manchester Central train and, simultaneously, a service for Wigan Central departs under Newton Road bridge on 24th October 1961. After nationalisation of the railways in 1948, ex LMS engines gradually made inroads into the services previously worked by the much older G.C. types. *Dr. J.G.Blears.*

Plate 34. In the late 1950s, the annual 'Station in Bloom' competition was won by Lowton St. Mary's and in this view the presentation is being made. Left to right are:- T.C.Byrom, District Passenger Manager, Liverpool Central; Stan Wood, Porter; District Operations Superintendant, Liverpool Central; gent in centre, unknown; Jimmy Atherton, Station Master; Tom Rigby, Porter and a Mr. Shufflebottom, Goods Manager, Warrington. After the closure of Lowton, Jimmy Atherton went to Newton-Le-Willows to take charge of the new Motorail Service.
Author's Collection, Tillotsons Newspapers Ltd.

Plate 35. A view of Lowton St. Mary's Station, also thought to be from the 1920s, showing the approach from Pocket Nook Lane on a very murky day. The clock says 11.40a.m. and the period advertisement below it is for Webb's seeds. *Author's Collection.*

Plate 36. Viewed from the northern side of Newton Road overbridge in the 1930s, the new signal box Lowton St. Mary's Junction, is seen on the left, details of which are given in *Fig 12*, and the redundant original on the right. The exact position of the bridge in the background can be seen in *Fig 11*, page 34.
Peter Hampson Collection.

Plate 37. Ex-War Department 2-8-0 No.90242 approaching Lowton St. Mary's on 29th May 1963 with a freight, possibly for Bamfurlong Sidings which the train would access via Amberswood West Junction and the Platt Bridge Junction lines.　　*N.Dyckhoff.*

LOWTON ST. MARY'S

Plate 38. Still in its London & North Eastern Railway colours, this station sign was salvaged from the station soon after closure.
Mike Whalley.

Plate 39. Another of the Stanier 2-6-4 tanks No.42432, is seen departing Lowton St Mary's with a service for Manchester Central on 16th May 1963
N.Dyckhoff.

37

Plate 40. Fairburn Class '4' 2-6-4T No.42235, stops at Lowton St Mary's with a Manchester Central - Wigan Central train on 17th May 1963. These engines were a development of the Stanier taper boiler design first introduced in 1945, ten years after the Stanier types. Note the cabin at the far end of the platform; it is thought that this originally housed the the first signalling levers for working Lowton Goods Yard. *N.Dyckhoff.*

Plate 41. On a dismal 23rd December 1963, Stanier Class '4' 2-6-4T No. 42601, arrives at Lowton St Mary's with the 2.15pm Irlam - Wigan Central workmen's train. *John Ryan.*

Plate 42. Seen at Lowton St. Mary's on 21st September 1963 is Class '4F' No.44501 with the L.C.G.B 'South Lancashire Railtour'. 44501 had taken over from Stanier '8F' No.48178 when the tour had reached Horwich Works and, by way of Hilton House, Crows Nest, Hindley No.2, De Trafford and Amberswood Junctions, gained access to the former Wigan Junction route. At Lowton the engine ran-round, worked to St. Helens Central and thence to Glazebrook West Junction and Manchester Central. *John Ryan.*

Plate 43. Giving a good view of the goods yard, this elevated shot at Lowton St. Mary's on 11th October 1964 is from the station steps as Fairburn 2-6-4T 42295 arrives with a Wigan Central train. Will someone help with the pram please! Now all this has gone, a timber company now occupying the site. *Peter Eckersley.*

39

Plate 44. Seaside excursions were to be seen with some regularity over this route having originated in the industrial heartlands of South Yorkshire and Nottinghamshire for example. On Saturday 23rd July 1961, B.R. Standard '9F' No.92115 passes through Lowton St. Mary's with 1M12 from Sheffield, an excursion to Blackpool and will access the Wigan (Lancashire Union) avoiding route at Amberswood East Junction, joining the W.C.M.L. at Standish Junction. These were the days when B.R. had plenty of stock to cater for such workings. It mattered not that this class of engine had primarily been built for heavy freight haulage as they were equally at home on passenger workings. They had, however, been limited to 60mph because of excessive speeds on other parts of the B.R. network.

Typical workings of these holiday specials in the early years after nationalisation routed via Glazebrook were:- 5.45am Desford - Blackpool North; 7.15am Newark - Blackpool North; 8.50am Sheffield Midland - Blackpool Central; 8.55am Leicester London Road - Blackpool North. Return workings were;- 8.55am Blackpool North - Leicester London Road; 9.25am Blackpool Central - Sheffield Midland; 10.25am Blackpool Central - Desford; 2.45pm Blackpool North - Sheffield. *Eddie Bellass.*

Plate 45. A view in August 2012, of the Lowton Station site looking south, now occupied by a timber yard. Hard to believe that excursion specials like the '9F' and its train shown above, once passed this way. If HS2 materialises, it will pass to the right of the timber yard. *Author.*

PLANK LANE

It is surprising that a station was built at this location at all, for at the time, there was nothing here; no housing as there is today, just a few cottages near the canal, some scattered farms and of course, a number of pit shafts and colliery railways. This was the area which, in the first instance, had attracted the railway companies to construct their lines hereabouts.

Upon taking the route at Glazebrook Junction the pleasant farmland would continue through Culcheth and Lowton for approximately 7 miles and even today, as viewed from Dam Lane, the abandoned trackbed still emits this air of tranquility. Arrival at Plank Lane though would have changed the passengers' conception abruptly as the eye was assaulted by the contrasting panorama.

As the mining industry followed the coal seams southwards from the Wigan area, new mines would be sunk and the topography of the landscape would be changed dramatically as the dirt tips rose skywards from the surrounding landscape. In a little under 2 miles between Plank Lane and Strangeways, the area became the most mined in the Wigan Coalfield and by the turn of the twentieth century, pithead gear, colliery railways, sidings and main-line connections abounded in every direction, only coming to an end with the closure of Bickershaw Colliery in 1992. Even all that is not the full story, for between 1975 and 1985 opencast mining took place on sites previously worked by Abram, and Diggles Higher Hall Collieries. At the time of writing, despite a clean-up at Plank Lane, most of the area is still a wasteland.

The locality was, at the time just outside the township of Westleigh, which in fact covers quite a large area in the Parish of Leigh. The area known as Plank Lane, (Plonk Lone to locals) was mostly, but not exclusively, on the northern bank of the canal, well populated and straddled the road on both sides of Plank Lane, itself an extension of Firs Lane, to the Leeds-Liverpool Canal.

It must be a matter of conjecture after all these years whether or not some unfortunate (or dimwitted) traveller actually booked a ticket from Manchester or Wigan, or from even further afield, to Westleigh & Bedford Station expecting to find himself in either of these two Leigh townships. On stepping onto the platform here what, I wonder, would have been his thoughts on seeing his surroundings! I'll bet he didn't make the same mistake again.

Plate 46. Westleigh & Bedford Station had obviously seen better days before this photo was taken in 1951. The station buildings lean drunkenly towards the platform which itself undulates alarmingly, mining subsidence being at the root of the problem. Just beyond the platforms the road into the goods yard and Bickershaw Colliery Sidings can be seen, the latter turning through 180 degrees in order to make a connection at Bickershaw Colliery. The name change from Plank Lane occured on 1st January 1894. *Author's Collection.*

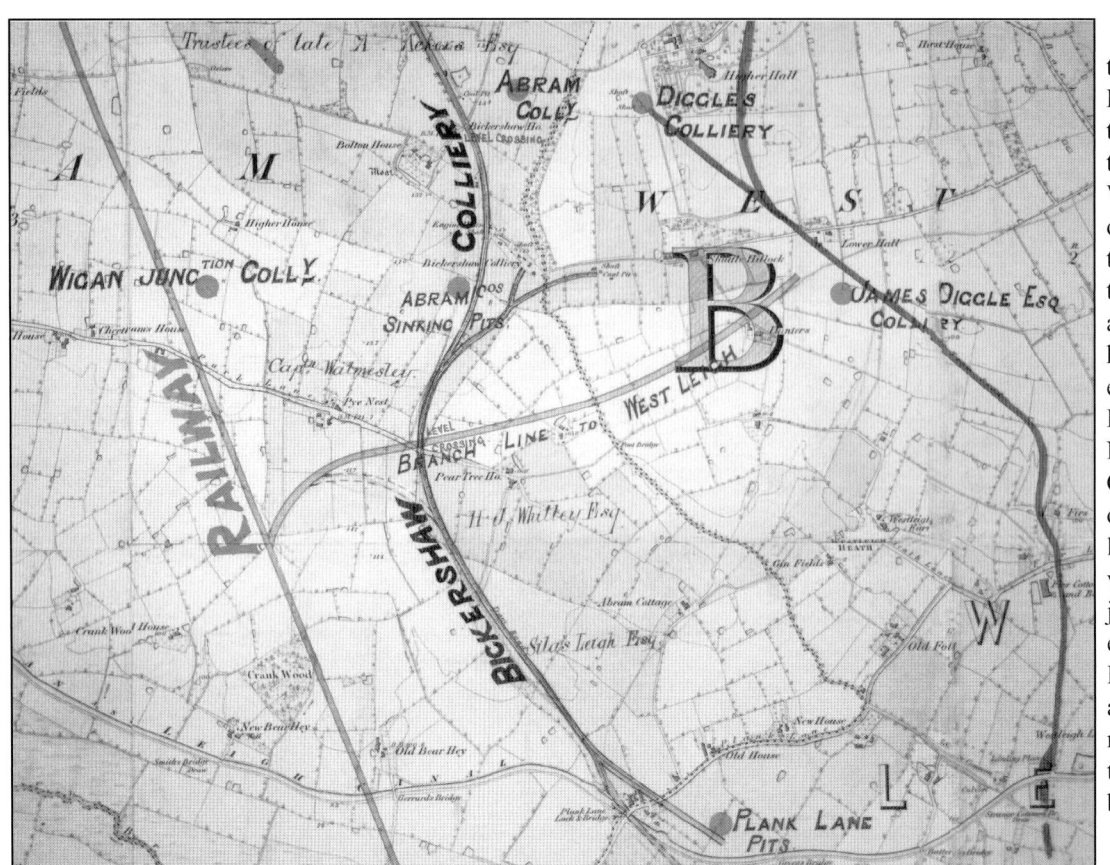

Fig 13. The amendment to the 1874 Wigan Junction Railways Act in the form of the Bickershaw Branch extension to James Diggle's Westleigh Collieries is seen on this original drawing, although no physical connection to Diggle's Branch is actually shown. It would have gone over the Ackers-Whitley Bickersaw Branch by a level crossing. Note that Wigan Junction Colliery would have been on the east side of the main line and the original, envisaged position of the junction to serve the Ackers-Whitley mines, and the Diggles pits, is shown at approximately 30 chains north of the centre line of the railway company's bridge over the canal.
Courtesy John Ryan.

Plate 47. This photograph of Crankwood Road overbridge facing eastwards, was taken on 1st September 1963. The steps for the Wigan platform at Westleigh & Bedford Station can be seen on the left, along with the photographer's father. As in all mining areas, subsidence was a reoccurring problem and the effects of it at Plank Lane are seen all to clearly as the left abutment of the bridge is now much lower than the right hand side. The station steps are still in situ but it requires a bit of searching through the undergrowth to find them.
John Ryan.

Plank Lane swing bridge which has, in early 2012, been rebuilt, also has an interesting history.

Originally, there had been a lock here, on the Abram side, and a fixed, shallow arched bridge. Mining subsidence dictated that it was no longer required and the first swing bridge, hand operated, was opened in 1910 along with a new footbridge for pedestrians. In 1934 the swing bridge was lifted by 18 inches and the footbridge by 5ft to counter the effects of further subsidence. In 1958 the bridge was again subject to overhaul, now operated by electricity and in 1973 the bridge was again rebuilt. In 1977 a completely new bridge was built to a design originating in Holland known as a Bascule Bridge. This was a lifting type of bridge rather than a swinging type.

North of Plank Lane Station was Park Lane level crossing and signal box. Here also was an unadvertised halt for workmen's trains from Wigan Central. Collier's trains ran from Moss Hall to Low Hall before the main line opened, possibly to the Wigan Junction Colliery in 1880, and certainly to the Ackers - Whitley's mines in 1892. There may have also been a small ticket office sited here so that miners who, not having obtained a ticket going on shift, could get one for the return journey at ½d which, if my maths is correct, equals 0.2 of one new pence.

The miners' trains are thought to have ceased using Park Lane Halt by the mid 1930s by which time the Ackers-Whitley mines had closed but the level crossing here was still in use until 1959.

In recent years much work has been carried out at Plank Lane to remove the scars left by the demise of the mining industry. In April 2011, a large 'Marina' was opened for the use of pleasure craft, a far cry from the days when barges laden with coal departed for Runcorn and, until 1971, for Westwood Power Station at Wigan. New roads have been made and the collection of Public Houses namely the *Britannia, Packet* and *Correction Inns,* and the hotch-potch of derelict buildings and scrap metal deposits which gave the area the long neglected look, demolished. It certainly looks far better now than it did.

Some 600 houses are planned to be built, along with an 18 hole golf course and part of a new access road from Smith's Lane, Bickershaw, for the latter, has been built but at the time of writing the large dirt tip remains as a visual reminder of Plank Lane's past history.

I have lived within sight of all of this for nearly fifty years; opencast mining has come and gone, yet the area north of Plank Lane is a wasteland, a residue of industry, forgotten and unloved. Will it ever change? Maybe, one day.

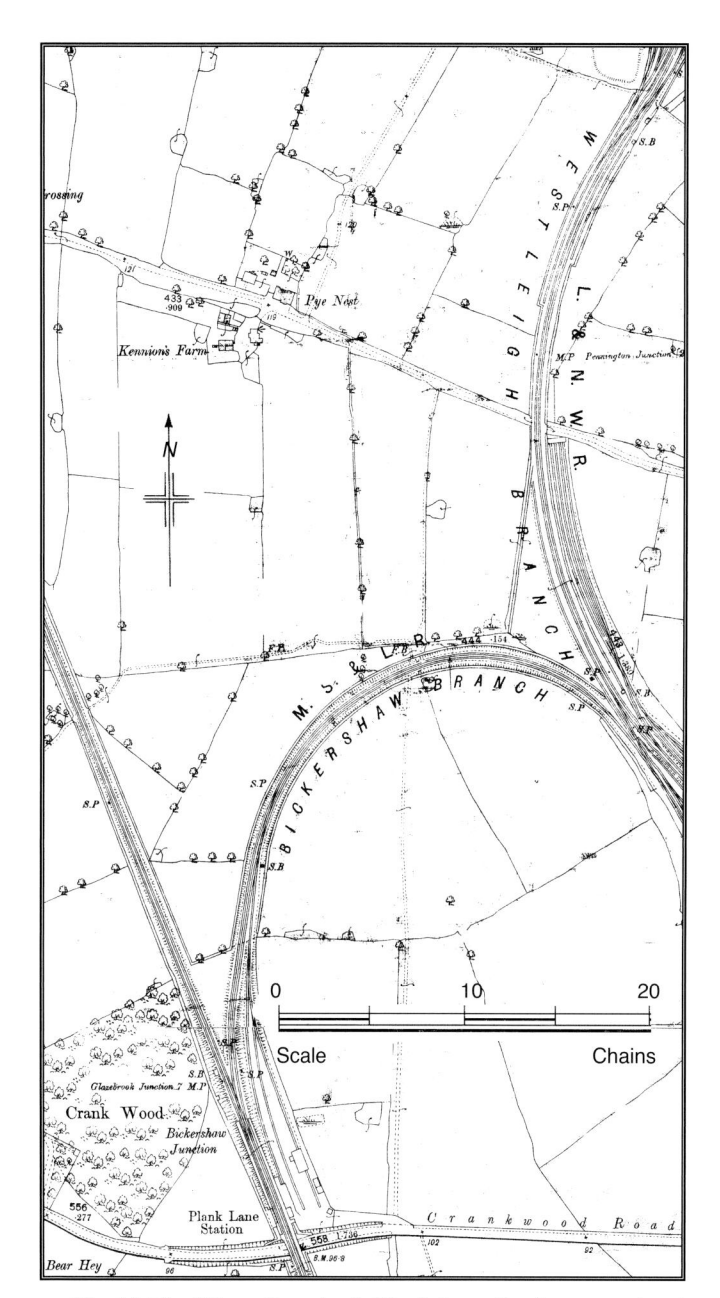

Fig 14. The Wigan Junction's Plank Lane Station, associated goods yard and Bickershaw Branch connections from the second series Ordnance Survey are shown here as built. Note 'Crank Wood', a name more commonly associated with the area today and the absence of any connection to the Abram Coal Company's mines at this period.

Of particular significance is the position of the Wigan Junction Railways' Bickershaw Junction which has been moved southwards, nearer to the Leigh Branch of the Leeds-Liverpool Canal giving a much longer lead into the curve and this is noticeable by its juxtaposition in relation to Crank Wood, as in *Fig 13* opposite.

Documentation held at Leigh Archives gives precise details of this and other amendments to the various proposed connections at Plank Lane as per the Wigan Junction Railways 1875 Act.

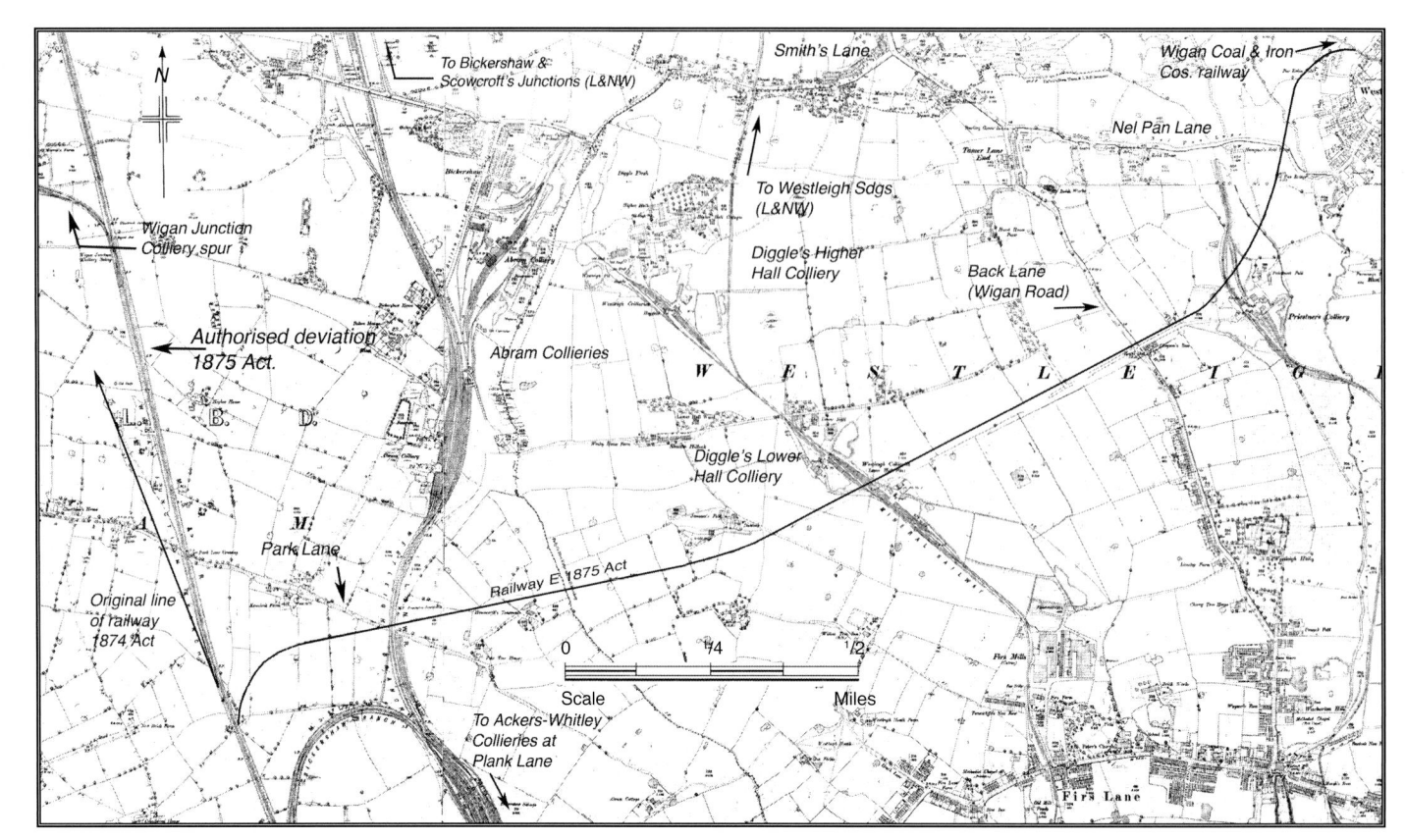

Fig 15. Here, Railway E of the 1875 Act, is overdrawn on the second series Ordnance Survey. This would have begun at approximately 30 chains north of the centreline of the bridge over the Leeds-Liverpool Canal, Leigh Branch at Plank Lane and, in part, from Bickershaw Junction, took the course of the branch to Diggle's railway as in the 1874 Act. Its course, roughly North-East, would cross the former Ackers-Whitley Branch near where the latter crossed Park Lane, thence crossing Diggle's Colliery Railway, and Wigan Road Westleigh, then known as Back Lane.

Diggle's railway had connections with the London & North Western at Diggle's Sidings, west of Hindley Green Station and later, at Pennington, just north of Pennington South Junction after the London & North Western had purchased the Ackers-Whitley private railway, making it into a through route between Pennington and Bickershaw Junction. Although Diggle's Collieries had closed in the mid 1940s, many of the outbuildings survived until 1975 when opencast mining operations began on the sites.

Curving in a more northerly direction, Railway E passes north of Priestner's Colliery and over Nel Pan Lane and loops eastwards to make a junction with the Wigan Coal & Iron Company's Railway 3 chains west of where the latter crosses Westleigh Lane at Fox Robin Fold. The connection to Diggle's Colliery authorised by the 1874 Act has been dropped altogether. The original line of railway, as per the 1874 Act, Railway No.1, has been amended between Plank Lane and the point where it approaches the Lancashire Union Railway at Amberswood by a maximum deviation of 1 furlong at Bickershaw Lane, the length of deviation being approximately 2 miles. It seems likely that the original line would have impeded the sinking of mines at Low Hall by the Moss Hall Colliery Company. The effect of this deviation meant that Wigan Junction Colliery's mines Nos. 1 & 2, the location of which are shown in *Fig 13* on the east side of the main line, would now be on the west side. The 1878 Act authorised deviations to Railway E, most notably to begin at $10^{1/2}$ chains from the canal overbridge for a distance of 2miles 2 Furlongs to Westleigh.

It will be noted from *Fig 15,* how many working mines were in operation in the mid 1870s in an area of approximately three square miles. Add to these the numerous old shafts, often unrecorded on the Ordnance Survey, that this was an intensely mined area.

The Wigan Junction Railways Act of 1878 authorised the Manchester, Sheffield & Lincolnshire Railway to bail out the former who were in some financial distress, not haveing enough resources to pay the contractors. The same Act also authorised some minor deviations to the Westleigh Branch, Railway E of the 1875 Act, extending it northwards to make a connection to the Wigan Coal & Iron Company's railway near Pickley Green, north of Westleigh Lane.

The Manchester, Sheffield & Lincolnshire Railway's New Works Act of 1881 were presented to Parliament in November 1880 and the following extract is reproduced from the *Manchester Guardian* of the 26th inst:-

A Railway No.1, commencing in the township of Abram in the Parish of Wigan, in the County of Lancaster by a junction with Railway No.1 authorised by the Wigan Junctions Railways Act of 1874, at or near a point on that railway distant $10^{1}/2$ chains measured along that railway in a northerly direction, from the centre of the bridge carrying that railway over the Wigan and Leigh Branch of the Leeds & Liverpool Canal and terminating in the township of Westleigh, in the Parish of Leigh, in the said County of Lancaster, at a point on the boundary between the townships of Westleigh and Atherton, distant 1 furlong 6 chains measured in a northerly direction along that boundary from the point where the Bolton-Leigh and Kenyon branch of the London & North Western Railway crosses that boundary.

This again refers to a Plank Lane - Westleigh Branch, which, in effect, was a deviation of Railway E of the 1875 Act, to make a connection with the Wigan Coal & Iron Company's Colliery Railway east of Priestner's Pit and Westleigh Lane. However, by the time this had reached Committee stage the plan seems to have been re-drawn to the effect of being extended towards Atherton to make a connection with Chanters Colliery at Hindsford, details of which will be found on pages 46-47. This was also objected to by the London & North Western Railway who already served Chanters by a branch line off the Wigan-Tyldesley route east of Howe Bridge. The matter went to arbitration and the branch was allowed although its route through Westleigh caused concern with the Leigh Local Board who raised a series of objections.

Plate 48. This is a view looking west towards the Turnpike from Bradshawgate, Leigh, in 1888, before substantial reconstruction of Leigh town centre began in the 1890s and early 1900s. The 1879 built Conservative Club on Railway Road can be seen and this was probably the only building to survive the coming reconstruction, as the main thoroughfares of the town were widened considerably. The point of interest, as regards the railways, is the M.S.& L.R. 'parcels receiving office' sign sited above the shop window, the proprietor of which must have been acting as agent for the railway company who would collect the parcels on a regular basis and take them to Plank Lane for onward transportation. After the arrival of the Wigan Junction Railway on the scene, intense competition for freight between the latter and the London & North Western is in evidence, the M.S.& L.R. as the operating company of the Wigan Junction Railway, doing all they could to entice existing customers of the North Western, to switch allegiance by offering cheaper rates and in many cases succeeding, Harrison -McGregor's farming equipment being the best example. *Author's Collection.*

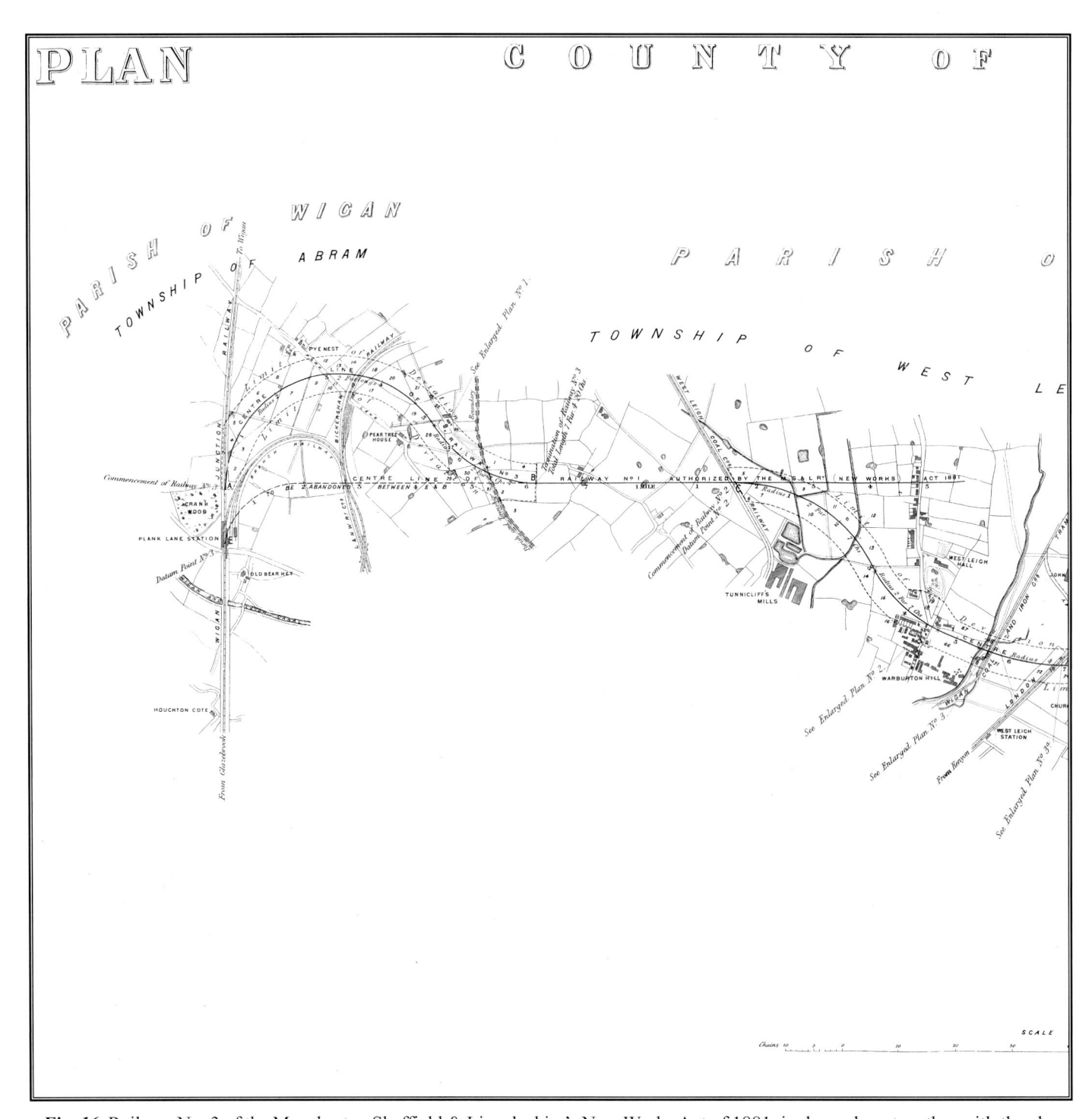

Fig, 16. Railway No. 3 of the Manchester, Sheffield & Lincolnshire's New Works Act of 1881, is shown here together with the abandoned section of Railway No.1 between points E & B and the authorised sections previously approved under the 1875 & 1878 Acts. The Authorised new branch, Railway No.3, would have run from a point north of the existing Bickershaw Junction at 10 1/2 chains north of the canal bridge through almost 180 degrees to connect with the remaining, previously approved course of Railway No.1 west of the Ackers-Whitley Branch, then running due east crosses Diggle's Westleigh Colliery Branch to meet Railway No.2. From there, Railway No.2 loops south-west to cross Wigan Road at Peacock Fold, over the Wigan Coal & Iron Comany's Railway which ran from their Westleigh Collieries southwards to Springfield Basin on the Leeds-Liverpool Canal, Leigh Branch, at Twist Lane. Railway No.2 then bridges over the London & North Western's Bolton-Kenyon line north of Westleigh Station. The extension of Railway No.1 beyond its connection to Railway No. 2 is believed to be a cartographers mistake. In the event, the 1881 Act went to arbitration before the Railway Commissioners and alterations made to placate the London & North Western who had opposed the plan.

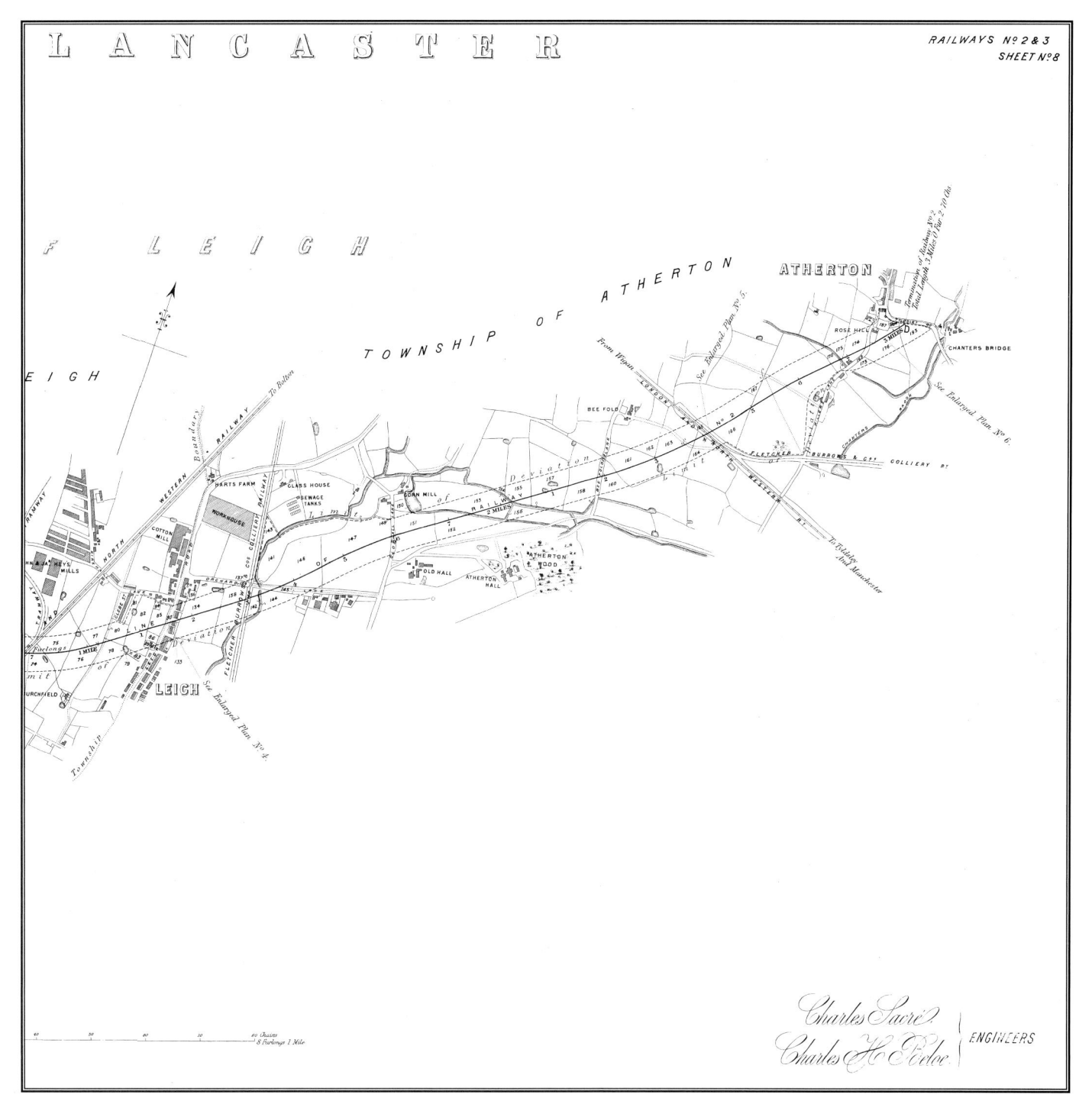

Next, as Railway No.2 begins to curve north-east, it crosses Church Fields, where terraced housing on Glebe Street has only recently been constructed, and Leigh Road, just south of its junction with Kirkhall Lane. Railway No.2 now crosses Fletcher's colliery railway which ran south from Howe Bridge Collieries to Bedford Basin on the Bridgewater Canal at Leigh, opening in 1857. This was in fact a replacement for an earlier Fletcher's railway which had run from Atherleigh on the Bolton & Leigh Railway to a landsale yard on Irvine Street, Leigh (off Leigh Road). Still continuing north-east, the railway burrows under the London & North Western's Wigan-Tyldesley Branch west of Chanters Sidings and in quick succession, crosses Millers Lane and Tyldesley (Old) Road, to terminate at Chanters Bridge, Hindsford, where connections would be made with Chanters Colliery, a total route mileage of 3 miles 60 yards. The 1883 proposal referred to on page 31 would use a similar route from Westleigh to Atherton. *Courtesy, Tim Oldfield.*

Plate 49. The view from a passing, Wigan bound train, hauled by Stanier 2-6-4T No.42664 on 23rd June 1962. The connections to Bickershaw Colliery have been lifted for some time but much of the track remains in situ, as does the ex G.C.coach on the curve.
Eddie Bellass.

Fig 17, below. This updated Ordnance Survey is taken after the grouping in 1923 and the L.N.E.R. Sidings are clearly indicated, entering the pit yard from top left passing under the former London & North Western's Bickershaw Branch lines.

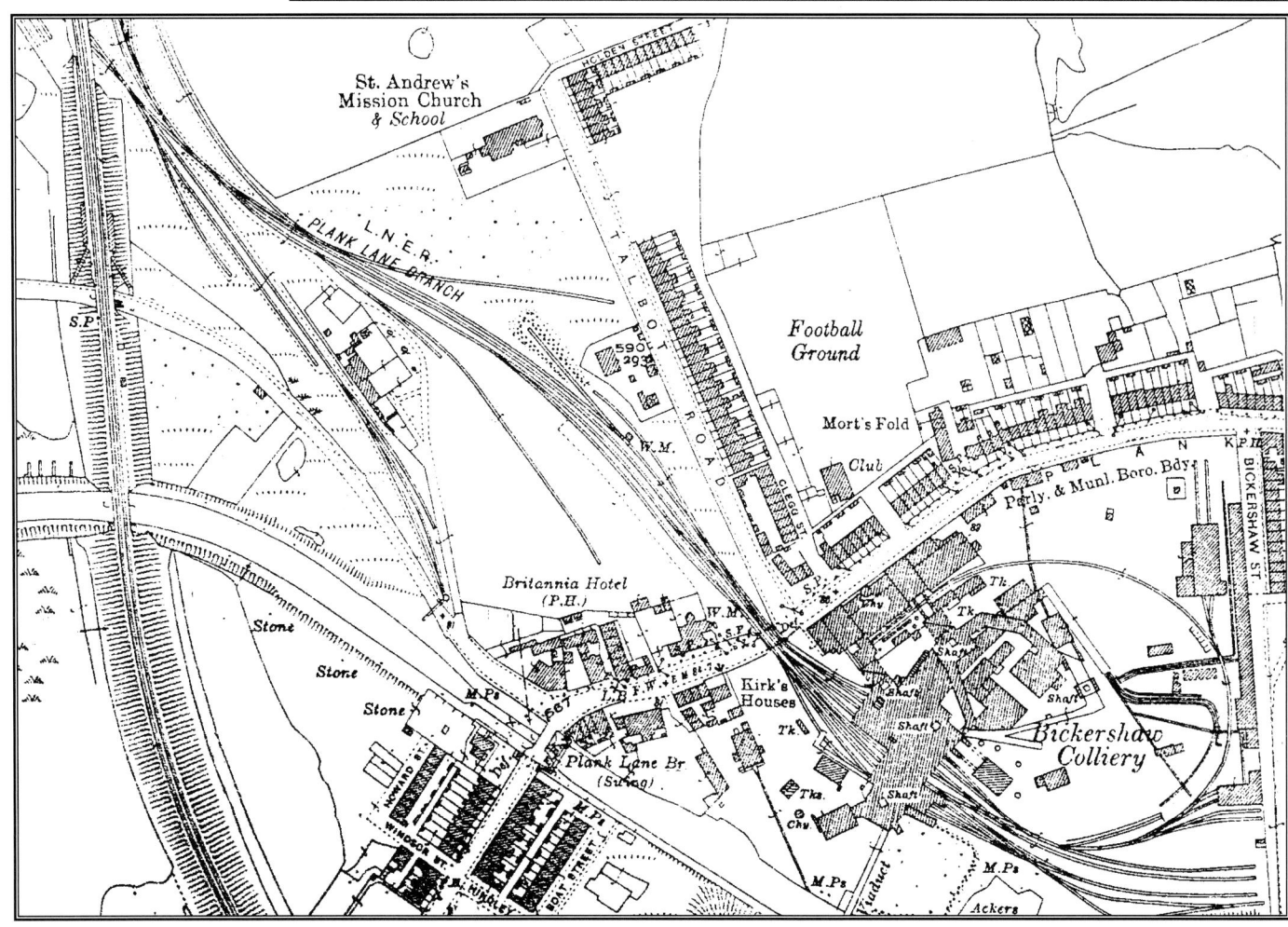

Plate 50. On 20th September 1964, an unidentified 2-6-4T engine calls at Westleigh & Bedford with a Wigan Central train. Now I wouldn't be surprised if some local collector still has the station bench, seen left, in his backyard.

Dr.J.G.Blears.

Plate 51. The Mayor of Leigh, Counc. W.Morgan, eighth from left, has a word with Mr. W.Haydock, conductor of Bickershaw Colliery Band prior to their departure from Westleigh & Bedford Station in 1937 for a band contest at Alexandra Palace, London. In previous years the contest had been held at Crystal Palace but this was destroyed by fire in 1936. Working left to right are; Bill Gregory, H.Jackson; Joe Gregory, Alf Coultas, W.Dawber, W.Haydock, the band's Conductor, J.H.Nicolls the Vice Chairman of the band, Mayor W.Morgan; the two gentlemen wearing spectacles are unknown. On the far right are Joe Nightingale and, wearing the bowler, W.Fogarty, the Secretary. The band had been formed in 1919 as Abram Colliery Prize Brass Band and after the amalgamation of Ackers-Whitley and Abram Collieries in 1933, the band was re named in 1937 to reflect the new ownership. *Author's Collection.*

Plate 52. This view at Plank Lane (LNER) Goods Yard dates from c1925/30 showing Class 'J10' No.5126 and its train made up of L.M.S., N.E. and L.N.W. wagons loaded with farm machinery from Harrison & McGregor's works at Leigh ready for departure. The engine is facing northwards and will draw forward before reversing onto the main lines. The curvature of the lines to Ackers - Whitley Colliery Sidings can be determined by the line of fence posts, the footbridge and the stationary wagons, centre. Working left to right the collieries are - Abram Nos.1 & 2, Abram Nos. 4 & 5, Diggles Higher Hall and Diggles Lower Hall. Nos. 1 & 2 would later become Albert Colliery and from 1975 to 1985 was the Opencast Executive's rail dispatch point for coal extracted from the Bickershaw opencast site which worked the area previously mined by Diggles Higher Hall and Abram Collieries. In 1933 the Abram Coal Co., and Ackers - Whitley Collieries would combine to form Bickershaw Collieries.

In 1939, two freights ran to Godley, the 12.15am from Westleigh & Bedford and the 6.20 from Wigan. In addition freights ran to Trafford Park Sidings and Warrington. Other trip freights went only as far as Glazebrook. About the same period there was a daily Westleigh - Bamfurlong Sidings freight and return working.

Author's Collection.

Plate 53. Shortly after passing through Westleigh & Bedford, the Westleigh distant is photographed from the same train, 42664, as seen in **Plate 49**. *Eddie Bellass.*

Plate 54. B.R.Standard Class '4' No.75051 arrives at Westleigh & Bedford Station on 20th September 1964 working to Wigan Central. Again, note the undulating platforms caused by mining subsidence. *Peter Eckersley.*

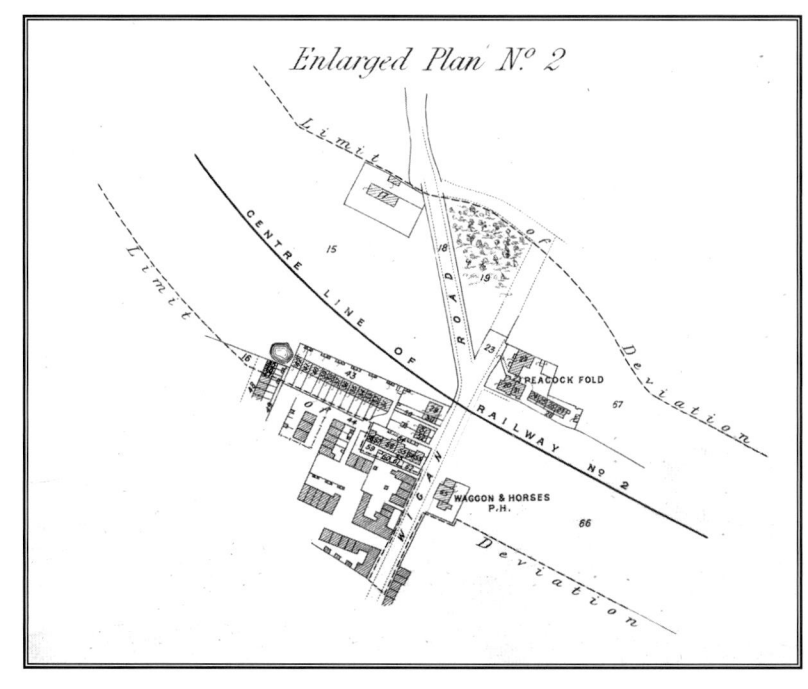

Fig 18. Enlarged detail from *Fig 16* of Plan No.2, of Railway No.2 of the Manchester, Sheffield & Lincolnshire Railway's 1881, New Works Act from Plank Lane to Atherton is shown at the junctions of Wigan Road and Peacock Fold. Here, Wigan Road would have been lowered by 2ft-6in to allow the construction of an arched overbridge with a span of 40ft and embankments at 15ft high on either side of the road. Nearby is the Waggon & Horses Public House.

Ticket, courtesy Tom Sherratt.

51

Plate 55. A view northwards from Westleigh & Bedford Station c1951. The lines curving away to the right went to Bickershaw Colliery forming a complete semi-circle where connections were also made with the London & North Western's lines from Bickershaw Junction. Note also, behind the signal on the curve, an ex-G.C. coach, minus bogies, in use as a bothy or store. The signal box, as seen here, is one of the Railway Signalling Co's. installations which presumably opened in 1884 when passenger services began from Darlington Street on 1st April. The box at Plank Lane Sidings dates from the same period.   *W.S.Garth.*

Plate 56. Bickershaw Colliery is seen from the junction of Crankwood Road and Plank Lane in October 1992. All of this has now gone, the roads re-aligned, and today, as you come over the canal bridge the road is level and the marina occupies the sites of the pubs seen here on either side of the road. It will be noted that the winding ropes to the pithead have been removed ready for demolition.
Author.

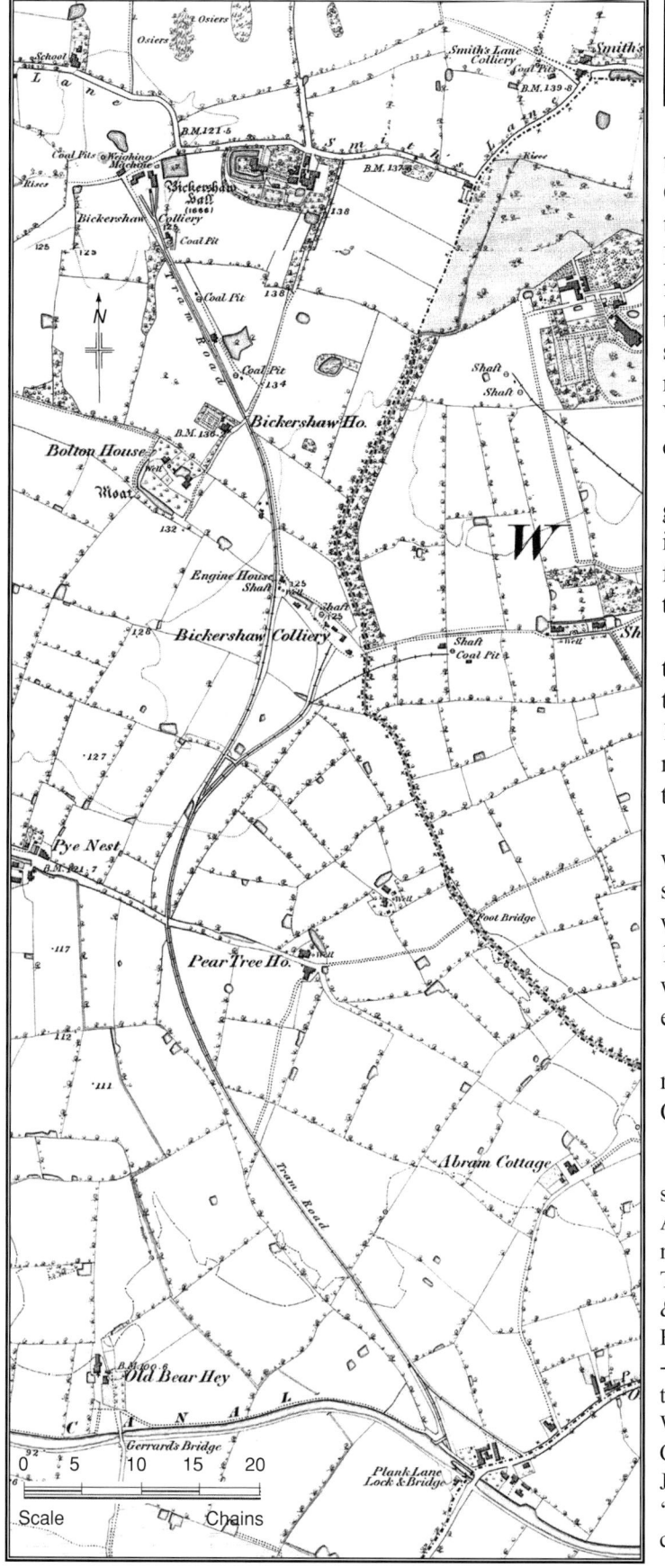

ABRAM AND BICKERSHAW COLLIERIES

Mining had begun in the area around Bickershaw Hall in the 1830s by Turner, Ackers & Co., becoming Ackers & Co. in 1842. In the late 1830s, a tramway was built from the original mines to the Leeds - Liverpool Canal at Plank Lane with a passing loop near Bolton House. By 1844 the firm had become Ackers - Whitley & Co. and had, over the years, sunk twelve shafts in the area between Bickershaw Hall and Park Lane. Mining activity though was moving southwards towards deeper seams and Ackers - Whitley & Co. began to concentrate their efforts nearer the canal.

By 1859, the tramway had been converted to standard gauge, locomotive working, as reports in the local press indicate a series of 'tests' being carried out with an engine fitted with mirrors enabling the driver to see the rear of his train when on the move.

A financial reconstruction of the Company in 1872 led to the formation of Ackers-Whitley & Co. Ltd., and work on two new pits began in the same year, and a further two in 1877 and, in the early years of the twentieth century, a fifth mine had been sunk and was in production by 1912. All of these new mines were sited near to the canal at Plank Lane.

In 1870s, only three of the original Bickershaw Collieries were still working and these were leased to Heyes & Johnson who sank two new shafts to work the deeper seams and widened the old No.3 ventilation shaft. On 12th March 1892, the Abram Coal Co. Ltd was formed. These mines were already connected to what had now become the Bickershaw Branch of the London & North Western Railway.

To connect with the Wigan Junction Railways, an agreement was signed on 23rd May 1892 between the Abram Coal Company Ltd. and the Manchester, Sheffield & Linc

Fig 19. The first series Ordnance Survey of the mid-1840s showing the early 'Bickershaw Collieries' opened out by Turner, Ackers & Co. and their tramway running from Bickershaw Hall, near Smiths Lane, to the Leeds - Liverpool Canal at Plank Lane. This tramway would, in the 1880s be purchased by the London & North Western Railway, upgraded and extended northwards to Bickershaw and Scowcroft's Junctions on the Wigan -Tyldesley - Eccles route opened in 1864, and southwards to Pennington on the Bolton - Kenyon line; a direct response to the opening of the Wigan Junction Railway in 1879. Note the absence of Crankwood Road, not constructed until the arrival of the Wigan Junction Railways to give access to their station. Note also 'Plank Lane Lock and Bridge', at the time a fixed bridge, becoming a swing bridge about 1910.

olnshire Railway, authorising a connection from Abram Nos. 4 & 5 pits to the Plank Lane Branch of the Wigan Junction Railways, constructed and paid for by the colliery company up to the Wigan Junction Railways' boundary, the railway company completing the installation. These works are believed to have been completed later in the same year. Colliery locomotives worked their own trains to the sidings.

Section 9 of the agreement states that:- *If the coal company fail for three months at any one time to send traffic over the branch railway the railway company to be at liberty to take up the branch.*

Although No.3 (ventilation) shaft was closed in 1916 the other pits continued in production until the 1930s. In February 1933, the Abram Coal Co. Ltd., and Ackers Whitley & Co. Ltd., amalgamated to form Bickershaw Collieries, the Abram Nos.1, 2 & 4 pits being formally abandoned in May 1933, No.5 being abandoned in June 1934.

A review made in 1941 by the LNER decided to retain the branch owing to the possibility of the colliery being re-opened. However, the Sidings List states that the colliery was dismantled in 1946, although some of the colliery buildings were not demolished until 1948. A recommendation made, and approved in 1948 was, that considering that they (BR) owned a portion of the sidings as per the original 1892 agreement, two sidings should be retained at an estimated annual maintenance and renewal cost of £106/1/7d, for marshalling traffic from other collieries and cripple storage. I personally interviewed a former LNE driver some years ago and he remembers working over the connection to these sidings in the early 1950s. **Plate 55,** clearly shows the connection still in situ c1951, although the rails are rusty.

The level crossing at Park Lane was out of use by 1959 and it is believed the connection at Westleigh & Bedford Station to the former Abram and Bickershaw Collieries was removed at the same period.

The former London & North Western's exchange sidings at Abram North remained in use until 1984/5 when new facilities at Bickershaw Colliery were commissioned.

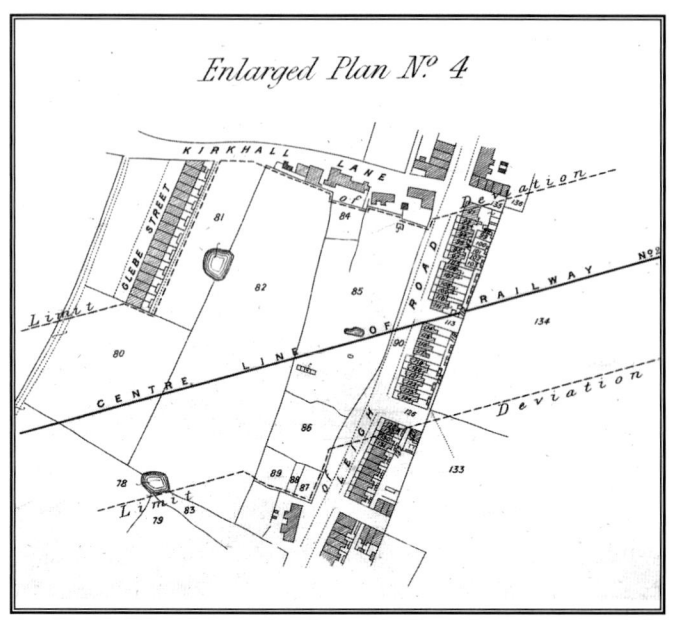

Fig 20. Enlarged detail of Railway No.2 from Plank Lane to Atherton, Chanters Colliery, authorised by the Manchester, Sheffield & Lincolnshire Act of 1881. Here, a 16 ft high, arched bridge having a span of 45ft would have crossed Leigh Road as the railway made its way to Atherton. From Plank Lane the railway is on a continuous embankment of 2½ miles until it nears the London & North Western's Wigan-Tyldesley Branch at Chanters Sidings where a tunnel would take the railway beneath the Tyldesley lines. At this point, an incline of 1:65 takes the railway over higher ground to reach its destination.

The houses on Leigh Road have only been built a year or two previously and Glebe Street is only partially constructed. Yet, here was a proposal which would have seen new properties demolished to make way for a branch railway which was, to say the least, hardly needed.

Plate 57. Two ex-London & North Western locomotives were purchased by Abram Coal Co. in 1881 and 1892 respectively. These had originally been built at Crewe in 1852 as 2-4-0 tender engines and in 1870, rebuilt as 2-4-0 tank engines. This is believed to be the second of the pair to have arrived at Abram, originally No.293 *QUICKSILVER*, works No.225/1852. It does not appear to carry any colliery identification number.
Author's Collection.

Plate 58. This photograph, which dates from 1954, is taken from the 1940s-built screening plant at Bickershaw Colliery. The London & North Western's Pennington - Bickershaw Junction route comes into the picture, upper left, and crosses over firstly, Crankwood Road and secondly, the former Wigan Junction lines by the overbridge, centre. To complement the new screens, a new bank of sidings have been laid from which access to both the former Wigan Junction and London & North Western routes is maintained. The new engine shed straddles some of the old sidings, bottom left. The train of wagons are thought to be 'cripples' from Abram North Sidings en-route to Earlestown Works. Recently, in 2011-12, Plank Lane and Crankwood Road were re-aligned and now cut through this area as part of an extensive reclamation project which has seen an impressive marina built on the north side of the Leeds-Liverpool Canal at Plank Lane.
Author's Collection.

Plate 59. Bickershaw Colliery Sidings c1908 with a variety of private owner wagons mixed in with the Bickershaw wagons. These are the colliery sidings on the northern bank of the Leeds-Liverpool Canal, Leigh Branch and the four headgears are of those shafts sunk between 1872 and 1877.
John Ryan.

Further developments, however, were to take place at Plank Lane. A new screening plant was built on the north side of Plank Lane and skip winding introduced at No.4 shaft in 1939, the first example in the country. Much of the colliery railway and sidings were realigned which largely remained intact until 1984 when a rapid dispatch bunker replaced the ageing infrastructure and a new overhead conveyor system transported coal straight from the pithead to the new bunker for direct loading into M.G.R. trains for Fiddlers Ferry Power Station worked throughout by B.R. locomotives making the previous arrangement of working coal trains to Abram North Sidings by colliery engines redundant.

At this juncture, the single track from Springs Branch to Bickershaw had been relaid throughout with welded rail and the gradient to Abram eased to facilitate the new method of working at a cost of some £8 million. Any remaining colliery trackwork at Abram North, including the lines from the former Nos.4 & 5 pits which, even at this late period were still in situ between the colliery site and Park Lane, were lifted.

Coal production at Bickershaw seemed secure for many years to come with the construction of these new facilities. This, however, was not to be, as the disastrous coal review of the 1990s saw Bickershaw and Parsonage Collieries closed in March 1992. Thus ended 160 years or more of coal production in this area of the Lancashire Coalfield.

Plate 60. Austerity 0-6-0 *Hurricane*, HE/3830/55, is seen climbing to Abram North Exchange Sidings with a loaded train from Bickershaw Colliery in August 1974. *Hurricane* along with *Spitfire,* HE/3831/55, had arrived new at Parsonage Colliery in late September 1955.

At this period there were still remnants of track from Abram Nos 4 & 5 pits hereabouts and the former through lines of the London & North Western's Pennington - Bickershaw Branch. All the trackwork still here, and at Abram North, would be lifted when the new layout for a rapid despatch bunker was built in 1984.

Author's Collection, (D.Jones).

Fig 21, right. Westleigh & Bedford Station and the surrounding coalfield are seen from this mid 1926 Ordnance Survey revision. At this period, railway infrastructure in the area was at its greatest extent given the number of mines in the locality. On the right is the London & North Western's Bickershaw branch which ran from Bickershaw and Scowcroft's Junctions on the Springs Branch - Eccles route, to Pennington South Junction. Initially, this had been the Ackers-Whitley 4ft gauge line from their Abram pits to the Leeds- Liverpool Canal at Plank Lane which had been converted to standard gauge by the late 1850s. In 1864, Ackers - Whitley extended their line northwards to meet with the short Scowcroft's branch line therefore gaining a connection with the London & North Western at Scowcroft's Junction.

In the mid 1870s, Ackers-Whitley concentrated their mining activity near the canal at Plank Lane and their Abram collieries were leased to Hayes & Johnson who began to trade as Abram Coal Co. in 1873, becoming a limited concern in March 1892.

As a direct counter to the arrival of the Wigan Junction Railway in the area, the London & North Western would purchase the Ackers - Whitley Branch in 1881, and by extensions to Bickershaw Junction and Pennington, have a valuable through route. As will be seen in *Plate 58,* the main London & North Western lines to Pennington run over the Wigan Junction lines by an overbridge. Note also the now disused London & North Western's Plank Lane Station. In the middle is Westleigh & Bedford Station and the associated goods yard and sidings. Upper left is Maypole Colliery showing its connections to the Wigan Junction Railways south of Park Lane Level Crossing and Park Lane Halt, the latter for use only by miners' trains. Note also that the Wigan Junction lines now have a connection to Abram Collieries Nos. 4&5 pits, built by the colliery company themselves under an agreement with the Manchester, Sheffield & Lincolnshire Railway of 23rd May 1892. The position of Plank Lane Sidings Signal Box is also shown.

57

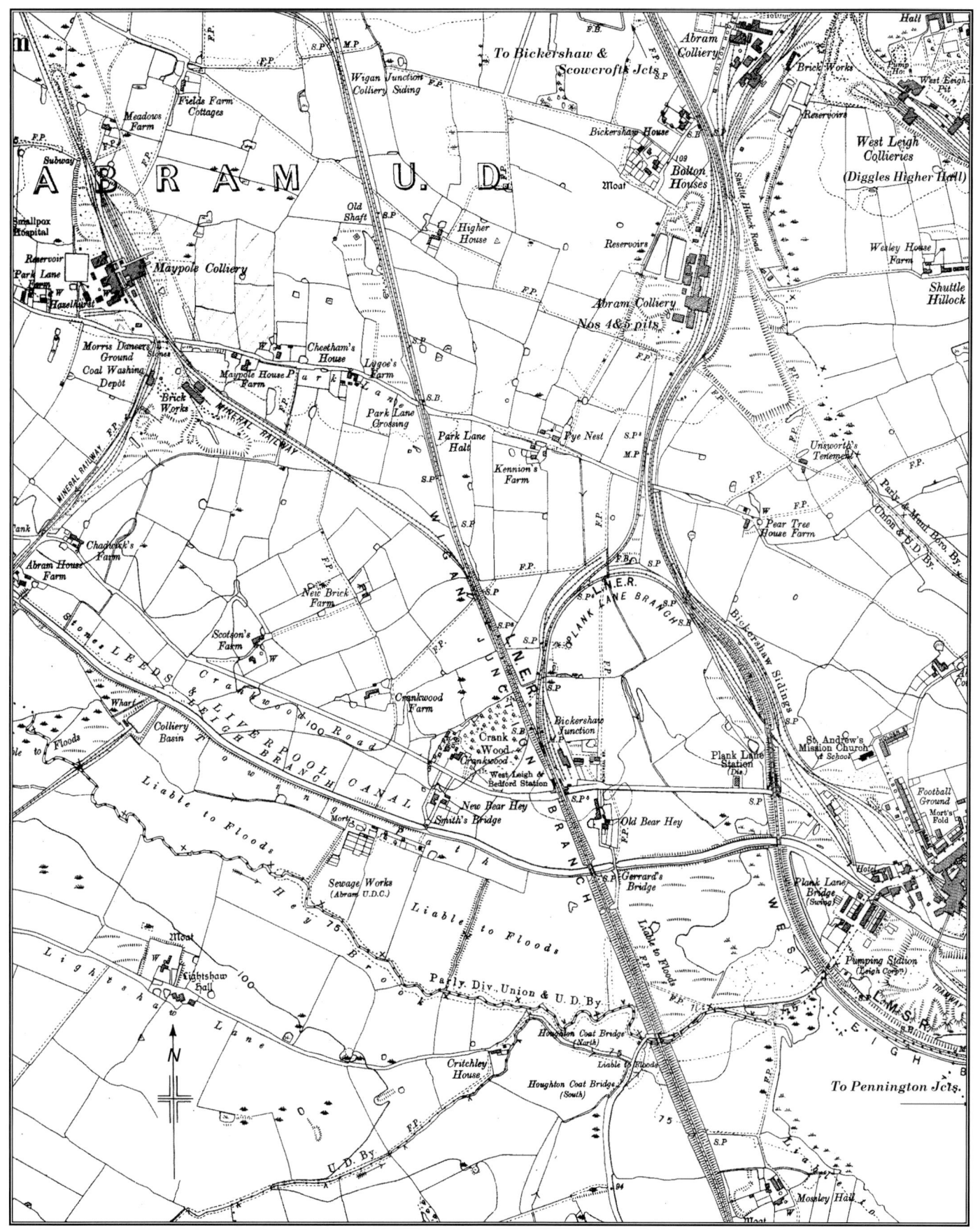

MAYPOLE COLLIERY

Preparatory work had begun on connections and colliery lines for Maypole Colliery, about a mile south of Low Hall, in early1895 and the first sod cut on the site on 24th April 1895. The Sidings Schedule reports that mainline connections from Maypole to the Wigan Junction Railways had been provided under an agreement of 1st April 1896. The mine was sunk by the Moss Hall Coal Company and started production in 1905, the Company's colliery railway from their Brookside pit (part of the Low Hall complex of mines) being extended, via the Wigan Junction Colliery, to the Maypole pits, necessitating the construction of a bridge over Bickershaw Lane, completed by September 1905.

Pearson & Knowles acquired a controlling interest in the Moss Hall Collieries in 1907. Shortly afterwards, on 18th August 1908, 75 men and boys were killed in a underground explosion and only 3 men escaped the devastation via an underground connection to Wigan Junction Colliery. Over the next few years the remains of the unfortunate victims continued to be found. The price paid for the winning of coal was indeed a heavy one. Under the new management, a branch line, running in a south-westerly direction, was built to the Leeds - Liverpool Canal, Leigh Branch offering alternative arrangements for coal transportation.

Plate 62. 0-6-0 ST *Delia* at Maypole Colliery on 24th November 1955. *Delia*, along with stablemate *Dorothy* had been built by Peckett & Sons of Bristol arriving new on the Moss Hall system in 1908 as replacements for much older and less powerful locomotives.
John Sloane Collection (F.D.Smith.)

Plate 61, left. The aftermath of the disaster at Maypole following the explosion at the colliery on 18th August 1908.
John Ryan.

Maypole Colliery was to close in 1959 but the connections off the former Wigan Junction lines remained until 1965 to serve the Wigan Junction Colliery and the Landsale Yard at Low Hall. Like other collieries in the area, Maypole became part of the Wigan Coal Corporation in 1930. Its chimney, however, became an isolated reminder of the hard won coal deposits of the area, not being demolished until 2006. Some of the outbuildings survive as industrial units and other parts of the site are now occupied by new housing.

WIGAN JUNCTION COLLIERY

North of Park Lane Level Crossing were the connections to Wigan Junction Colliery which had been formed on 1st October 1875, by Wm. & John Turner, who had sunk two shafts, pits Nos.1 & 2, near to Park Lane Level Crossing.

Work was commenced on No.1 shaft on 5th June 1876 and after a relatively easy start through clay, sand and gravel, a bed of sandstone was encountered at a depth of 38 yards. Boring operations thus began and the sandstone was found to be 65ft yards thick, with copious quantities of water. No.2 shaft was immediately started, passing through the sandstone at 100 yards deep. Pumps were then installed to begin pumping to the surface. It had been envisaged that the sinking of No.2 would assist with the dispersal of water from No.1 shaft.

A tunnel had been driven under the sandstone connecting the two shafts and a lodge constructed to hold the water. Sinking recommenced, almost with disastrous consequences, when on 20th December 1876, whilst the workmen were drilling plug holes in the sandstone for a brick ring, water burst through the stone and into the shaft.

Abandoning their tools, in a hurry, the men were raised clear in the hoppet. The water rose up the shaft to within 56 yards of the surface and despite the two large pumps of 16in diameter working at a much higher speed, pumping out 2,000,000 gallons a day for a month, water levels were only reduced by 4 yards. It was at this point that Nos.1&2 were abandoned.

Such was the disincentive of this disaster that in 1877 the company was almost wound up. However, fortitude prevailed, and the sinking of Nos. 3&4 pits began in 1878 on a site further north which proved more successful, production beginning in 1880.

Concomitantly with the sinking of Nos.1&2 pits, connections had been made to serve these under section 27 of the Wigan Junction Railways Act of 1875 and it appears that a signal box was built at Park Lane to control colliery access and the level crossing.

However, with the failure of Nos 1&2 shafts it had been intended, by an agreement of 25th February 1884, to relocate the Wigan Junction connections further north, as this would be more convenient for pits 3 & 4. Two short sidings are shown in *Fig 22 below,* with a connection to pits 3&4 and it is presumed that these were worked, in the early years, by a ground frame until a signal box was installed here in 1884.

On 9th February 1884 the signal box at Park Lane was abolished and the original connection for Wigan Junction Colliery's 1&2 pits removed and a new box opened for

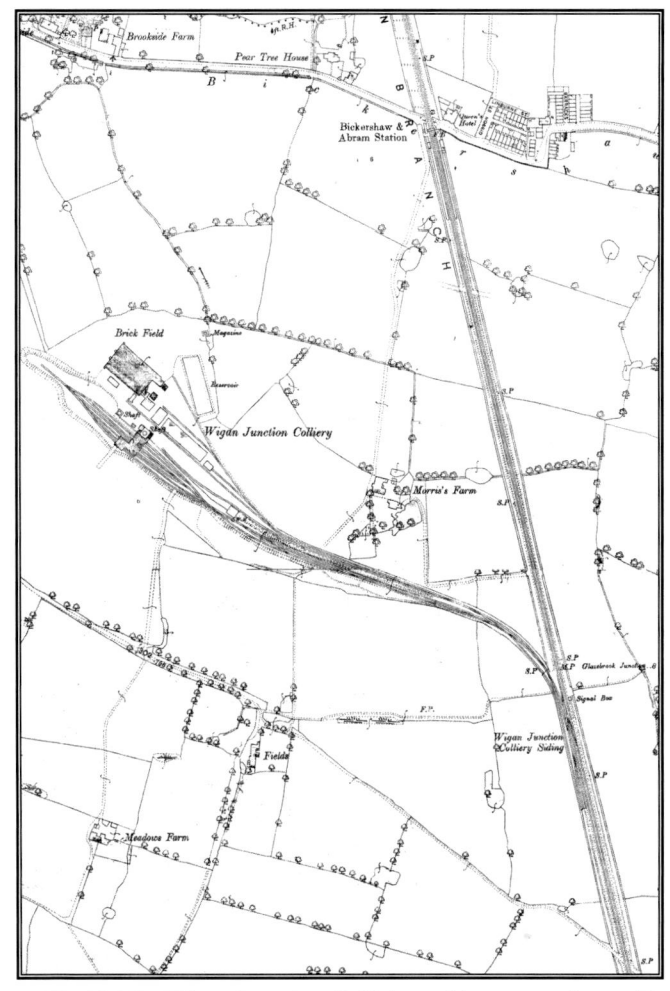

Fig 22. The Wigan Junction Colliery and its connections with the main lines are shown here on this second series Ordnance Survey from 1892, before it was connected to the Low Hall and Maypole pits in 1905. The signal box shown here at this location was inspected on 9th February 1884.

pits 3&4 at the northerly location, together with new access/egress crossings. However, further track alterations were carried out in 1894 including, it is believed, an extension of the Wigan Junction Colliery Sidings towards Park Lane and the reinstatement of pointwork for mineral workings. s*ee **Fig 21**.

Yet more alterations were carried out, as by 25th June 1908 the Wigan Junction Colliery box was abolished and replaced by a ground frame, inspected on 19th February 1909. The signal box at Park Lane had been reinstated to control the southern access to Wigan Junction Colliery.

With regard to Nos. 1&2 pits, all was not lost, as on 1st November 1879, Wigan Junction Colliery entered into an agreement with the Wigan Union Sanitary Authority for the supply of 150,000 gallons of water per day from the flooded shafts for a term of 40 years at 6d (2.5p) per 1,000 gallons.

In 1907, Pearson & Knowles acquired a controlling interest in the Wigan Junction Colliery and, as already mentioned, the Moss Hall Collieries. Although these collieries continued to trade under the former names, railway operations were streamlined on close cooperation.

A reorganisation of the mining industry occurred in the 1930s due to the depression in the coal industry. The Pearson & Knowles Coal & Iron Company and their subsidiary concerns, together with the Wigan Coal & Iron Company and Partington Steel & Iron Company were to amalgamate. The iron and steel manufacturing plants became the Lancashire Steel Corporation centred at Irlam on the banks of the Manchester Ship Canal, allowing their much older works at Kirkless and Warrington to be closed. The amalgamated collieries became the Wigan Coal Corporation.

The branch line connection to Wigan Junction Colliery from Park Lane was used only intermittently by 1946 and the northernmost connection giving access to the loop removed. The branch provided under the 1874 Act to Low Hall was removed about the same time, all inward traffic now using the connection to Maypole Colliery, the wagons shunted to wherever on the system they were required by colliery engines.

It appears though that the long siding northwards from Park Lane and the connection into Wigan Junction Colliery was still in situ as, by an agreement of 18th January

Fig 23. Detail of the Agreement between the London & North Eastern Railway and Wigan Coal Corporation c1946 regarding the new pointwork off the loop line to allow colliery trains from Wigan Junction Colliery access to the tipping grounds set up on the former site of Wigan Junction's Nos.1 & 2 collieries. As can be seen, the northern connection to the loop has been removed.

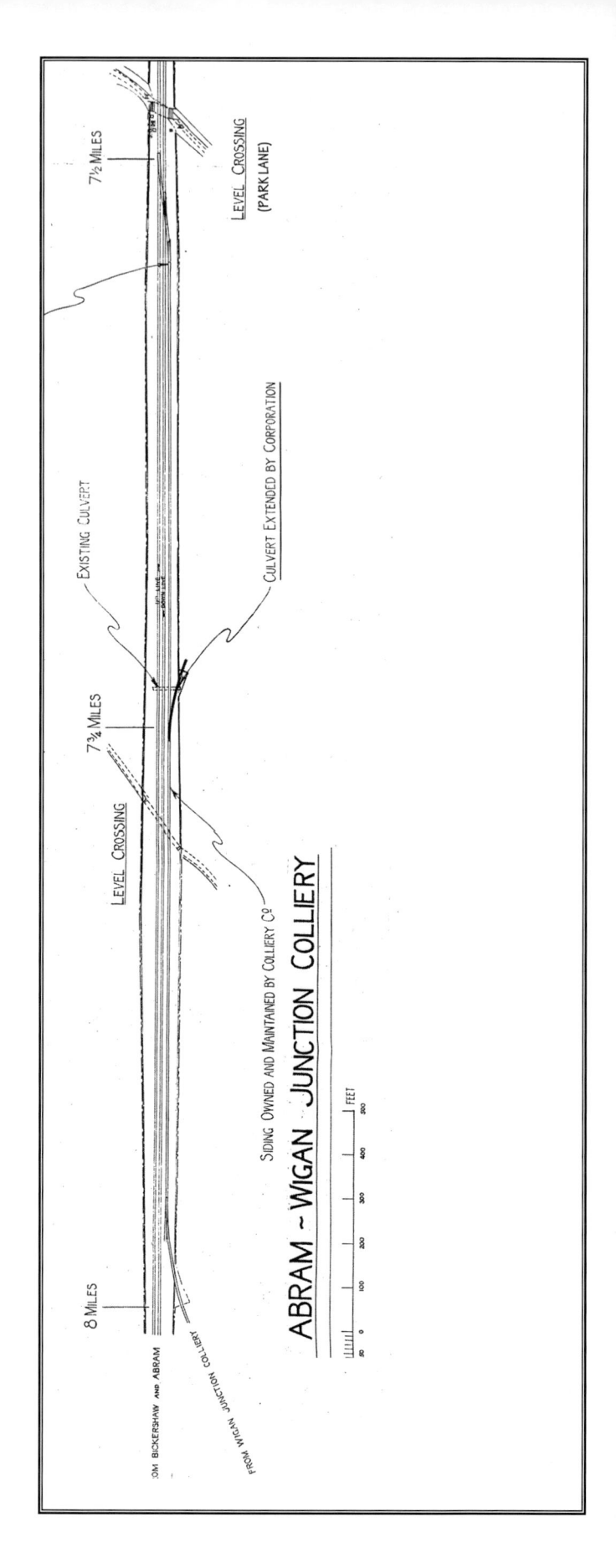

1946, the Wigan Coal Corporation had agreed to take over its maintenance, with the Railway Company supplying any materials required to keep it in "good repair" and, a new south facing, gated, sidings connection had been laid off the loop about ¼ mile north of Park Lane for use as a tipping ground for colliery waste from Wigan Junction Colliery on the site of the original Nos.1 & 2 pits.

At nationalisation of the mining industry in 1947, the former Moss Hall Colliery railway from Ince via Amberswood to Low Hall, its extensions to the Wigan Junction and Maypole collieries, and to the Leeds-Liverpool Canal, Leigh Branch, were still in use but connected only to the main lines by the former London & North Western link at Bickershaw and the original Wigan Junction Railways connection to Maypole.

However, on 11th April 1956 the National Coal Board wrote to the London Midland Region, of which the former Wigan Junction Railways were now a part, that: *we agree that the siding connection* (to Wigan Junction Colliery) *need not be relaid when the main lines are relaid and we undertake not to ask for the siding to be reinstated at some future date.* This refers to the 1884 agreement between the Wigan Junction Railways and the Colliery Company.

The engine shed at Low Hall closed in 1959, the two remaining engines, No.6 and *Daisy*, being transferred to the old loco shed at Wigan Junction Colliery which had been reopened. Wigan Junction Colliery was to close on 11th May 1962, Maypole having closed in 1959 but the connection here to Maypole was used to bring in coal from other collieries for the landsale yard at Low Hall until early 1965 when the depot closed. The branch connection to the former L&NW/LMS lines at Bickershaw was removed in 1966.

Plate 63. *Daisy*, an 0-6-0 saddle tank built by Pearson & Knowles Coal & Iron Co. in 1910 at their own, Dallam Forge Works at Warrington, is seen at Wigan Junction Colliery in August 1961. Along with *Dorothy* and *Delia*, these three engines provided most of the motive power on the Low Hall system. *Author's Collection, (Jim Peden).*

BICKERSHAW & ABRAM

Bickershaw & Abram were two distinct villages in the nineteenth century, with Abram some distance away from the station, but with an expanding population as more mines opened in the vicinity with new terraced housing being constructed along the main road at Abram between Bickershaw Lane and Dover Lock. (A573)

Bickershaw Village was much more compact at the time and the station within easy walking distance. Most of the cottages at Bickershaw were centered around Bolton House Road and Smith's Lane, the latter an extension of Bickershaw Lane, (B5237) and here the local church and school were, and still are, situated. In fact, early mining activity at Bickershaw was adjacent to Bickershaw Hall. *(See Ordnance Survey, page 53)*. In the twentieth century, with the exception of a new estate built opposite the church, new house building tended to be erected in a westward direction towards the station on either side of the main road, on the western side of the London & North Western railway bridge.

I can recall the local wakes week as holidaymakers from the village, carrying heavy portmanteaus, made their way along the footpath towards the station in the early 1960s. A sight that was soon to disappear forever.

Plate 64. On a fine summer's day, a six-car DMU passes over the level crossing at Bickershaw & Abram in August 1964 with a Manchester Central train. Far right is Hindley Prison, built in the 1960s near the former Victoria Colliery site. L.M.S. style upper quadrant signals have replaced the original Railway Signal Company installations.

The taking of the above photograph was the result of a question put to the Transport Users Consultative Committee (TUCC): that as the service was still run by steam trains could it be run more economically by diesel multiple units. The reply given stated there were not enough spare units available even to consider this! In due course the Minister of Transport consented to the withdrawal of passenger services on the appropriate date. On the Monday following consent the whole service was turned over to units - presumably the same units that were not available. The photographer took pictures of these 'non-available' units between Wigan and Lowton-St. Mary's and sent them to the TUCC, North West Area. Did it make any difference? No it did not and closure went ahead. In effect, this was just another example of the dirty tricks waged by officialdom.

Eddie Bellass.

Plate 65. A much earlier photo at Bickershaw & Abram than that seen opposite and below. The crossing gates still retain the original, square posts, signalbox nameboard and the sleeper fence. *C.H.Townley.*

Plate 66. On the last day of passenger services over the route, 1st November 1964, and having previously been photographed at Culcheth outward from Manchester, B.R. Standard Class '4' No.75057 rattles through Bickershaw & Abram with a return train from Wigan Central giving an impressive display of steam power. *Peter Eckersley.*

HINDLEY FIELD AND VICTORIA COLLIERIES

Hindley Field Colliery was situated to the north of Bickershaw Lane, Nos 1&2 pits on the east side of the Ackers - Whitley Branch, and Nos 3&4 on the west side. Nos 1&2 first appeared in the mines list in 1866, trading as the Bark Hill & Hindley Field Coal Company, becoming, simply, the Hindley Field Coal Company on 30th June 1872. Nos. 3&4 pits pits were sunk in 1880 and by manoeuvering over the Ackers - Whitley line, colliery locomotives were able to serve all the Company's mines.

Under the 1881 Act by which the London & North Western purchased the Ackers - Whitley lines, the Hindley Field Coal Company were permitted to cross these lines from one site to the other and section 10 of the Act allowed them to transport their coal to the Leeds - Liverpool Canal at Plank Lane.

J.E.Rayner had acquired control of the Hindley Field Coal Company Ltd., and Victoria Colliery, in 1899. Victoria Colliery was sited to the west of Hindley Field Nos. 3 & 4 pits and was first shown in the mines list for 1896 under the ownership of Victoria Coal Company. Ltd., under Rayner's ownership becoming the Victoria Colliery Company Ltd. The colliery was linked to the London & North Western's Bickershaw Branch via the Hindley Field Coal Company's sidings and also had a connection to the Wigan Junction Railways, put in by an agreement of 19th May 1903. This was sited south of the connections to Low Hall Colliery.

J.E.Rayner had running rights, using his own locomotives over the main lines of the Wigan Junction and the London & North Western Railways and could thus work his traffic from one colliery system to another.

The previous owner of Victoria Colliery Company, a Mr. Grundy, had arranged with the Hindley Field Colliery to work his traffic, having no locomotives of his own. In the event, the colliery was short lived, closing about 1910. The connection with what was now the Great Central Railway was retained to serve Hindley Field Collieries, the agreement for use transferred to the latter on 11th January 1911.

The last of the Hindley Field Collieries, pits Nos. 3&4, were to close in March 1927 and the agreement permitting the working of private trains over the Bickershaw Branch terminated as from 17th April 1928. The agreement concerning the former Wigan Junction connection had been cancelled on 30th November 1927.

In the post World War II period, more housing was built on the north side of Bickershaw Lane and, in the 1960s, Hindley Prison, which covered the site of Victoria Colliery and any remaining traces of the colliery railway that served it. Note also the, then, alignment of Bickershaw Lane, east of the station, which since has been realigned, taking out two 90 degree bends.

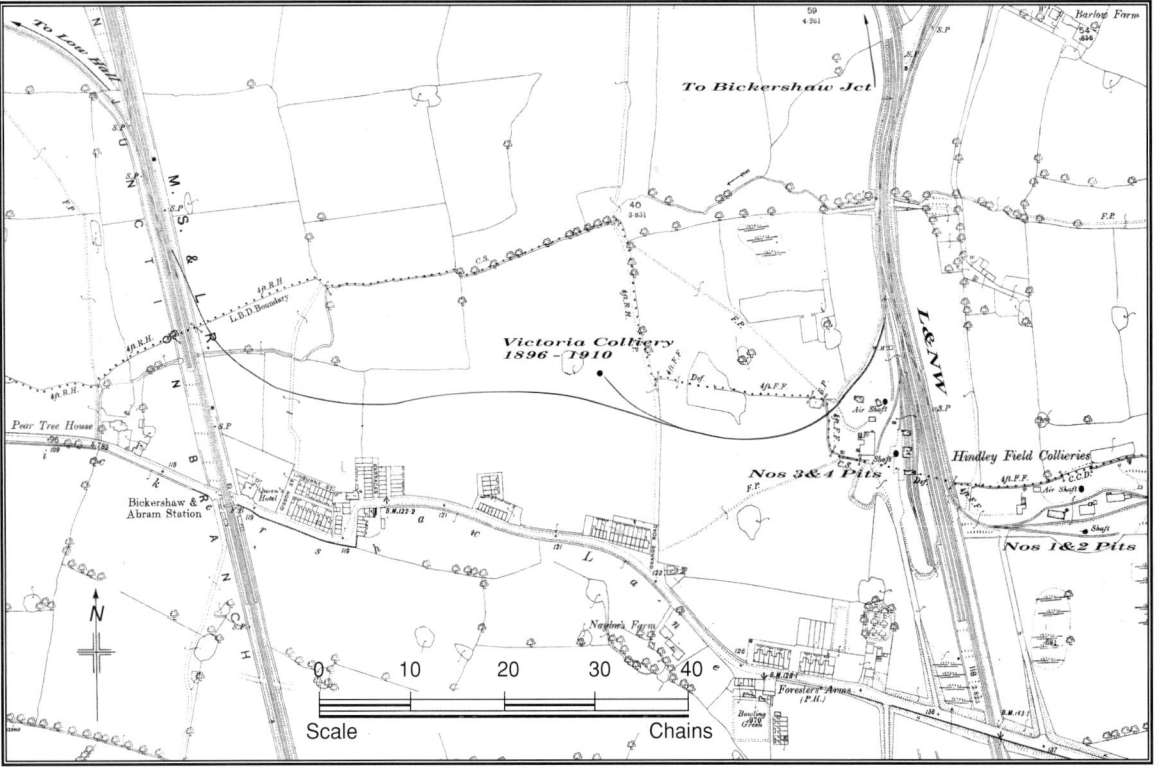

Fig 24. Hindley Field Colliery and the site of Victoria Colliery, with the approximate route between their connections to the Great Central and London & North Western Railways shown on this mid 1920s Ordnance Survey.

Plate 67. A misty day at Bickershaw & Abram as Class '4' Fairburn 2-6-4T No.42174 arrives with a five-coach train for Wigan Central on 31st October 1964. Time passes so quickly; these youngsters on the platform will now be in their early sixties and I can remember scenes such as this when I came to Leigh in the same decade, often passing this way. Maybe the service over this route could never have been described as exciting but the speed at which closures came, in four or five years, left whole communities devoid of rail transport and we are all so much the poorer for their loss. *Peter Eckersley.*

Plate 68. The 'Up' Manchester platform at Bickershaw & Abram as photographed in August 1964. The heading on the notice board says "Withdrawal of Railway Passenger Services." The 'booking office' leans towards the waiting room in dismay!

Eddie Bellass.

Plate 69. A good track view towards Westleigh & Bedford as the six-car DMU seen in *Plate 64* departs from Bickershaw & Abram in August 1964.
Eddie Bellass.

Plate 70. Ex-L.M.S, Ivatt designed 2-6-0 No. 46419, is seen between Bickershaw & Abram, and Hindley South in September 1964, running light engine in the Wigan direction. The newly-built Hindley Prison is in view top right.
Tom Sutch.

Plate 71. An unidentified 2-6-4T passing Hindley Prison on the approach to Bickershaw & Abram Station with a Wigan Central - Manchester Central service in August 1964. *Tom Sutch.*

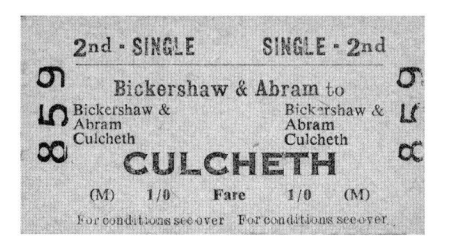

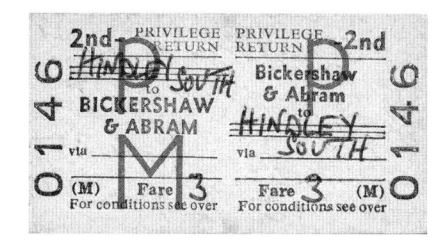

Tickets, courtesy, Tom Sherratt.

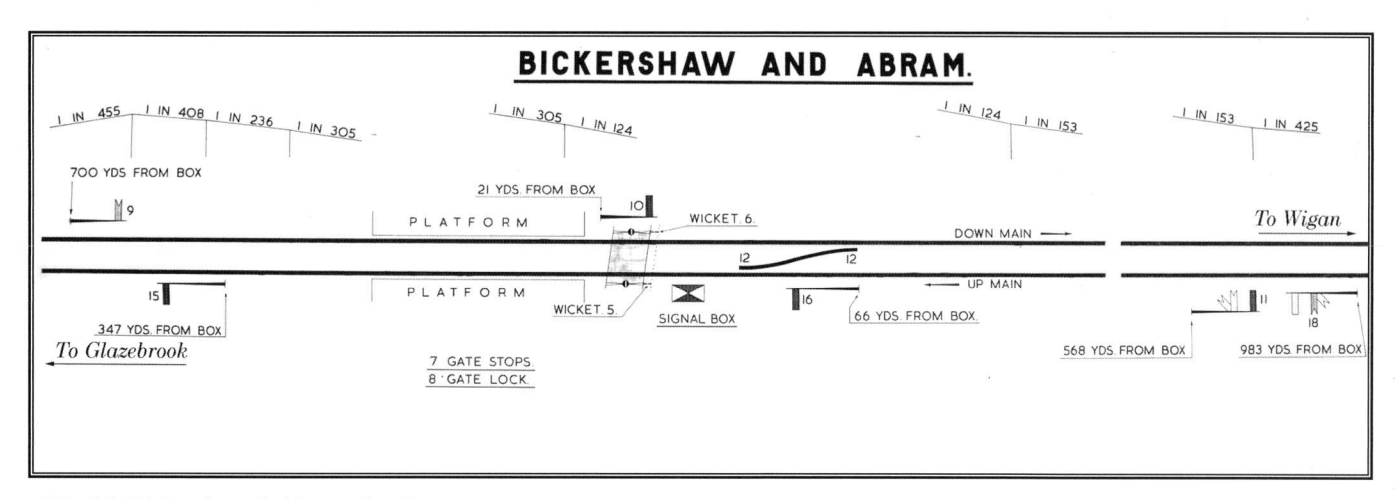

Fig 25. Bickershaw & Abram details. *Courtesy, Tim Oldfield.*

67

Plate 72. Working a Manchester Central - Wigan Central train, Stanier 2-6-4T No.42654, having passed Hindley Prison, is now about to pass, firstly, beneath the branch to Low Hall Collieries, and secondly, the Wigan - Tyldesley- Eccles route. The picture also gives a good illustration of the London & North Western's Hindley Junctions Railway from Bickershaw Junctions to Hindley & Platt Bridge. Most prominent feature in the background is Scowcroft's Tip, with, below that and slightly right, is Bickershaw Junction signal box. The 'Down' connection to Hindley & Platt Bridge (Hindley South from 1950) follows a clockwise semi-circle from Bickershaw Junction to pass under the main London & North Western lines, whilst the 'Up' connection comes in at top left, running towards the signal box at Bickershaw.

After the arrival of the Wigan Junction Railways on the scene a number of proposals were put forward to secure a connection with the London & North Western to Low Hall Collieries. Finally, under an agreement of 1st July 1886, the London & North Western were to construct a branch from Bickershaw Junction to Low Hall at its own expense, partly on its own land and partly on private land and this followed the course of the Hindley Junctions 'Down' line before deviating to cross into Low Hall by the bridge, left. The new branch was, however, to be regarded as the property of the Moss Hall Coal Company.

Tom Sutch.

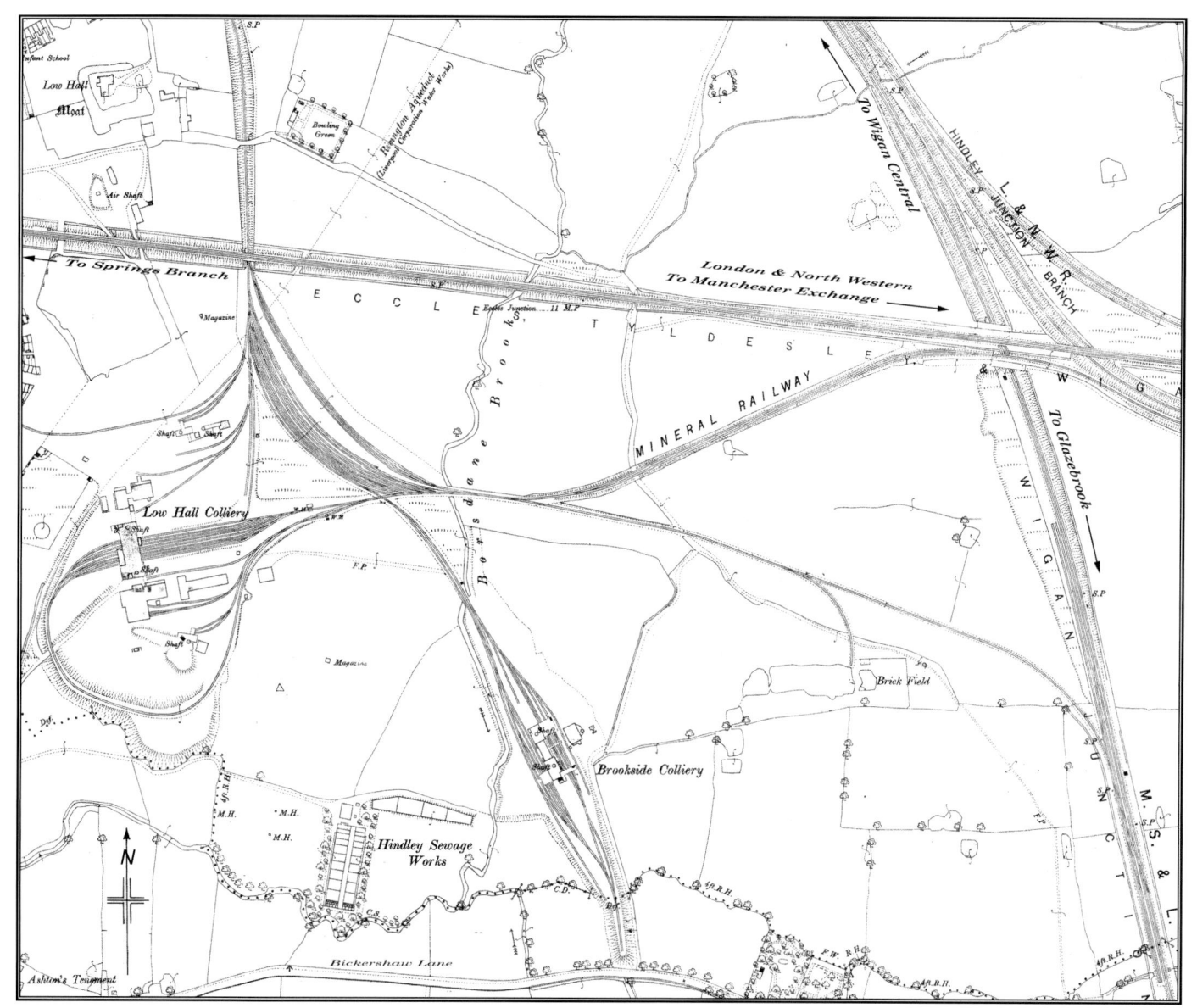

Fig 26. The second series Ordnance Survey showing the main lines of the London & North Western and Wigan Junction Railways to the north of Bickershaw Lane. Low Hall and Brookside Collieries are at the zenith of development and in 1905 the colliery railway would be extended across Bickershaw Lane from Brookside to connect with the new Maypole Colliery.

LOW HALL COLLIERIES

The Moss Hall Coal Company had been active in the area of Lower Ince from the 1830s. In the 1850s they opened up a number of small pits on the Low Hall Estate - Low Hall Collieries, near to Platt Bridge. The Moss Hall Coal Co. had links with the North Union Railway via the Springs Branch near Ince Forge, and with the Lancashire & Yorkshire Railway at Ince Station, their colliery railway crossing the Springs Branch at Ince Hall by a flat crossing as seen in ***Plate 165, The Wigan Branch Railway.*** The Moss Hall Co's. mineral railway was extended to Low Hall via Amberswood Common, opening about 1860. On 22nd May 1867, the Company became a limited liability concern and although their earlier mines at Ince continued in production until 1888, their main centre of production now were those mines on the Low Hall Estate. In 1873 the Moss Hall Co. Ltd. opened Brookside Colliery to the south-east of the Low Hall pits and the two sites were connected by the colliery rail system.

Haulage to their main line outlets on the Springs Branch, or to the Lancashire & Yorkshire connections at Ince Station from Low Hall, were though, becoming an inconvenience at a distance of some 2½ miles.

69

Section 27 of the Wigan Junction Railway Act of 1874, stipulated that a branch line was to be built from the Wigan Junction main lines to Low Hall and that the said branch was to connect with the London & North Western's Eccles - Tyldesley - Wigan route and all were to be built at the expense of the Wigan Junction Railways but could not become their property and, were to be opened not later than the opening of the main lines.

The Wigan Junction route opened on16th October 1879 and it is likely that the branch to Low Hall from the main lines also opened on the same date. It was certainly open by August 1880 as an accident is reported near the new sidings to the main line involving a company collier's train working to Low Hall. However, the connection to the Eccles-Tyldesley-Wigan route was not built, despite a number of proposals which included one by the London & North Western Minerals Manager at St. Helens. An agreement of 1st July 1886, authorised a connecting branch line to be built from Low Hall to Bickershaw Junction. The line was to be constructed by the London & North Western at its own expense, on railway and private land and worked by their locomotives, but be regarded as the property of the Moss Hall Coal Co. It seems likely that this branch was constructed concomitantly with the London & North Western's Hindley Junctions lines, authorised in 1883 and completed on 20th October 1886.

By 1892, considerable improvements had taken place at Low Hall, whereby the main winding shafts, pit Nos. 5 & 6, were connected to a new screening plant under which the empty wagons were propelled by a colliery locomotive to gravitate through the loading plant and by a circular internal railway layout, then drawn towards the main lines for despatch. It will be seen from the accompanying *Fig 26*, how this was accomplished by a well thought-out system of lines which also included connections to the London & North Western at Bickershaw Junction.

In 1895, preparations were being made for the sinking of Maypole Colliery, the first sod being cut on 24th April 1895. Connections to the Wigan Junction Railways of this new venture were provided under an agreement of 1st April 1896, production beginning in 1905 and the colliery railway extended from Brookside, by a bridge over Bickershaw Lane to serve it.

The Pearson & Knowles Coal & Iron Co. acquired a controlling interest in the Moss Hall and Wigan Junction Collieries in 1907, although the two companies continued to trade under their old names. At this juncture, a spur was built from the Brookside - Maypole colliery line to serve the Wigan Junction Colliery and a branch line built from Maypole to a new discharge wharf on the Leeds - Liverpool Canal, Leigh Branch. *See area map Fig 21, page 57.*

Sidings Schedules report that the former Moss Hall connection with the Springs Branch was removed in 1916 as, by now, the former workings at Lower Ince had ceased. The connection to the Lancashire & Yorkshire at Ince was retained and not finally abandoned until the 1960s.

In the early 1940s, all empties were put in at Maypole Sidings by L.N.E.R. engines and worked to Maypole, Wigan Junction or Low Hall Collieries by colliery locomotives, and outward traffic worked via Bickershaw Junction by the L.M.S. Interestingly, c1924, the Sidings Schedule records traffic for Abram and Hindley U.D.Cs. being worked in via the Bickershaw Junction route, and again in 1926, when contractors materials for new housing at Crankwood were being built for Abram U.D.C., and delivered to site by rail.

Plate 73. Built by Hudswell - Clarke & Co. in 1894, 0-6-0 No.5 is seen at Low Hall Colliery on 20th April 1952 during a visit by members of the Industrial Railway Society.
John Sloane Collection.

Plate 74. Shaft collapse at Brookside Pit on 30th April 1945. The shaft was the 12ft diameter, 334 yard deep New Zealand No.7 pit. As can be seen the colliery railway passed directly over the shaft which had been filled in c1932, presumably with pit dirt. The rails had been joined in the centre of the shaft. The loaded wagons of the train had dragged *Dorothy* and its unfortunate driver backwards as a chasm some 127ft deep opened up, cratering in line with the railway to 56ft, and across the rails to 34ft.

Plate 75. When the dust had settled loco *Dorothy* could be seen with buffers pointing skywards. Note how the shaft has collapsed inward on the right hand side and also the curbing rings of the shaft which were spaced about 20 brick courses apart. These rings were fixed to the strata and made either from cast iron or timber. It was not known if the locomotive and wagons had wedged in the shaft or were resting on top of the infill. The subsequent fire caused by the scattered firebox debris burned through causing *Dorothy* to fall further down the void.

Returning to the accident mentioned on Page 70, as reported by the *Wigan Observer*:- On Monday 8th August 1880, one Joe Houghton aged 30 was killed during a derailment. *The Company's train runs from Moss Hall to Low Hall and back each morning and evening. Trucks or carriages are provided. When the Moss Hall Company's train was approaching Low Hall Colliery where a siding branches from the main line to the new railway siding, something having gone wrong with the points, two of the front wagons went on the wrong line. The, points having righted themselves, the other wagons <u>kept to the main line</u>. The workmen, seeing what had happened, and apprehending the danger of remaining in the wagons which were being propelled by one of the Company's locomotives, jumped out. Before deceased could get out of the way one of the waggons fell over and killed him.*

Two facts are relevant here. Firstly, the train would have to travel to Low Hall by the collieries own private railway from Moss Hall, there was no other way. Secondly, that the wagons kept to the main line would seem to indicate that the train had worked beyond the mainline junction at Low Hall, perhaps to Wigan Junction Colliery which by this date was in production, and was returning to Moss Hall. If so, then the train would have gone over the level crossing at Bickershaw Lane, both on its outward and return journeys. No mainline passenger services were running until 1884 and, it is by no means certain that both the up and down lines had been completed *in toto*. One can only presume that colliers trains operated with the permission of the railway company.

One of the most unusual events ever to occur in British mining history happened at Brookside Colliery on 30th April 1945 when a locomotive, its driver and train of 13 loaded wagons plunged into a collapsing mine shaft which had suddenly opened up beneath the train.

The driver, one Ludovic Berry of May Street, Abram was, as usual, in charge of 0-6-0 ST *Dorothy*, a 1908 built engine purchased from Peckett & Sons of Bristol by the Moss Hall Coal Company.

Plate 76. In the late 1920s, driver Ludovic Berry is seen on the footplate of *Dorothy,* which, along with stable-mate *Delia* were 0-6-0 saddle tank locomotives supplied in 1908 by Peckett & Sons of Bristol, to replace an ageing stock of less powerful engines. *Author's Collection.*

Plate 77, below. Ex - Wigan Coal & Iron Co. 0-6-0 ST *Sultan,* seen at Low Hall about 1952. After nationalisation in 1947, engines which had previously worked only over their own colliery system were often transferred to other collieries as replacements for engines undergoing repair and the Kirkless Works became the main engine repair depot for collieries in the Wigan area. *Sultan* had been built in 1906 by Naysmith - Wilson at their Patricroft Works. It was to be scrapped at Low Hall in 1959. *Harry Townley.*

On that fateful day, Ludovic was shunting his train over the old 334 yard deep New Zealand shaft situated about 1/4 mile north of Bickershaw Lane. His brakesman, John Ward, was walking alongside the train as it began to be shunted into the siding. John noticed the shaft infill collapsing, leaving a gaping hole over which some of the wagons had already passed. A few moments later, the complete train, with Ludovic still at the controls plunged into the abyss with a deathly rumbling amidst a cloud of rising steam. The weight of the wagons had buckled the rails and dragged the rest of the train, and the engine, backwards. John shouted to Ludovic to jump clear but he stayed on the footplate trying to save his train by applying the locomotive's brakes.

The inquest into this accident was held at Abram Council Offices where it was confirmed that it had been New Zealand shaft, officially known as Brookside No.7 Colliery which had been opened in 1885, the last coal being wound in 1919. For some years the shaft had been used for ventilation until 1931 when approximately 8,000 tons of debris was used to plug it. The local mining agent said he had inspected the area the day previously and reported that all seemed well. He also mentioned the number of old mines in the area which, combined with recent heavy rain must be taken into account. It seems likely that underground water courses had washed away the bottom infill thus causing the collapse.

The shaft was filled in again sometime afterwards and, in the 1990s, despite the protestations of the family to try and recover the locomotive, and the drivers body, the Coal Authority drilled and grouted the top infill of the shaft.

A memorial now marks the site where Ludovic gave his life trying to save *Dorothy*.

The last of the Low Hall pits, No.5, closed in 1931 but the locomotive shed at Low Hall didn't close until 1959, along with the closure of Maypole Colliery, the former shed at Wigan Junction Colliery was reopened, being in a central position to work over the colliery rail system to the landsale yard at Low Hall which remained until 1965. The sidings agreement with British Railways in respect of the former London & North Western connection at Bickershaw Junction was terminated on 17th May 1965 and taken out of use by 31st October 1966.

STRANGEWAYS & HINDLEY

Here, the London & North Western Railway was to make connections with the Wigan Junction Railways; the former's plans for their Hindley Junctions Railways were submitted in 1882 and envisaged a completely independent set of lines from Bickershaw Junction, running alongside of the Wigan Junction's lines, to make connections with the Lancashire Union at Amberswood which had opened in 1869. However, the proposals were modified by the Parliamentary Act of 1883, which obliged the London & North Western to connect with the Wigan Junction Railways south of Hindley & Platt Bridge Station but granting running powers to the North Western over the Wigan Junction's lines to Amberswood East & West Junctions.

London & North Western notes give a signal box at Amberswood West Junction from 19th July 1880 which at this period probably controlled the Company's workings into Strangeways Hall Colliery, which they were entitled to work into free of any toll charges, granted under the Manchester, Sheffield & Lincolnshire Railway Act of 1879.

It was from this colliery that the first traffic over the Wigan Junction route to Glazebrook commenced on 17th October 1879. The previous day the line had been traversed by a 'Directors Special' consisting of an engine and three first class coaches which departed from a point just north of Stoney Lane overbridge enroute to Glazebrook.

According to the Sidings Schedules, Railway No.4 of the Wigan Junction Railways Acts, that is Strangeways West to Amberswood West Junction, (Amberswood South Curve) was completed in late 1882. It appears the trackbed of this curve was laid to ballast level by Crompton & Shawcross under an agreement of 1st October 1878, but the track laid by the Wigan Junction Company.

Under the same Act, Crompton & Shawcross were to construct a new access road to Strangeways Hall Colliery as their existing access would be taken up by the main lines, and with the assistance of the Railway Company's Engineer, divert Liverpool Corporation's Rivington Aqueduct which passed under the area to the north of Stoney Lane (now Liverpool Road) where embankments and bridge works would carry the lane over the new railway. The mining company would be paid £2,000 in respect of the work undertaken.

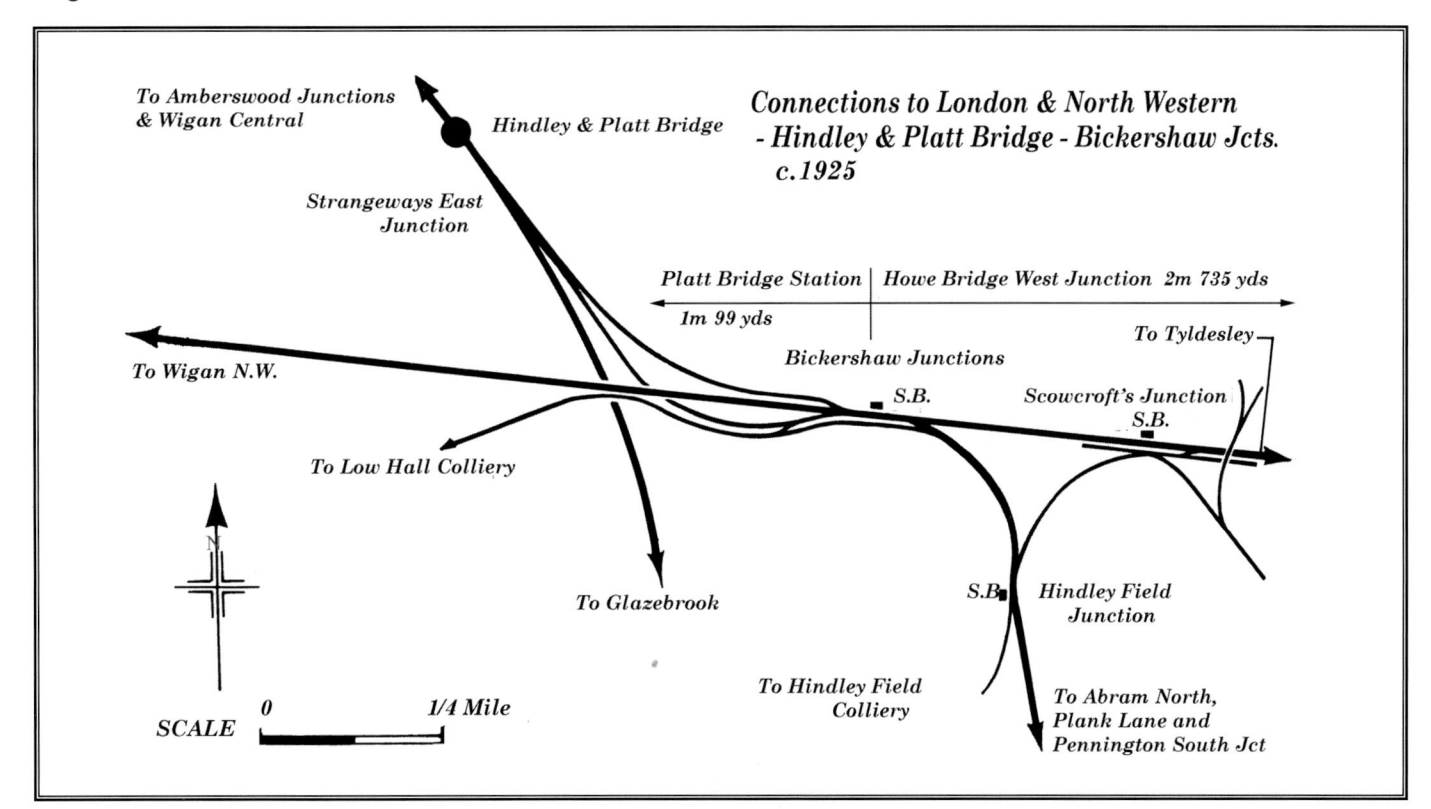

Fig 27. The Hindley Junctions Railway as instituted under the London & North Western Acts of 1883 and their connections to the Wigan Junction Railways are seen c.1925. Also shown is the connection into Low Hall Colliery, authorised by a separate agreement and probably constructed concomitantly with the Hindley Junctions lines.

73

Plate 78. Stanier 2-6-4T No.42634 calls at Hindley South with a Manchester bound train on 4th April 1964. Originally Strangeways & Hindley, the name changed on 1st January 1892 to Hindley & Platt Bridge, and again on 1st July 1950 to Hindley South. In this view the original Railway Signalling Co's. lower quadrant signals have been replaced by L.M.S. upper quadrants. See *Plate 80.*

Peter Eckersley.

A further Act of 1st October 1880 authorised a new connection to Strangeways Hall Colliery because 'certain difficulties had arisen'. A new lead into the colliery off Amberswood South Curve was provided which was to be constructed by the railway company and to be maintained by them. The new lead began under the occupation bridge and the sidings extended towards what is now Liverpool Road. Siding capacity at the colliery was also extended by three new marshalling sidings on the north-west side of the colliery.

The curve to Amberswood East Junction however, was far from being completed. The London & North Western's line plan for their Hindley Junctions Railway shows that some track had been laid on the Strangeways West - Amberswood East section (Amberswood North Curve) but had not been connected to the Lancashire Union Lines and, apparently, the Wigan Junction Railways being short of funds, were in no hurry to proceed.

A second signal box was opened by the Lancashire Union at Amberswood West Junction on 11th October 1886 and the signal box at Amberswood East Junction opened concomitantly, intimating that the curve from Strangeways West Junction to Amberswood East must have been completed. The Platt Bridge Junction Railway which connected with the Lancashire Union at Amberswood West Junction, was to open on 25th October. The Hindley Junctions Railway also opened in October 1886, the signal box at Strangeways East having been inspected on 11th inst., allowing the North Western through running over the Wigan Junction lines.

Crompton & Shawcross had taken over Strangways Hall Colliery in 1875. This is the same Strangeways Hall that had a connection with the North Union near Skew Bridge at Bamfurlong which would be removed prior to the quadrupling of the main lines in the 1880s.*

Following the opening of the Hindley Junctions Railway the London & North Western had at last a useful avoiding line to by-pass the congested through - Wigan main lines and whilst initially intended for freight, some passenger trains were routed via Hindley & Platt Bridge, and working by way of Amberswood North Curve gained access to the Whelley route. The first of these were through trains from Manchester to Blackpool which, from the summer of 1887, were directed via Bickershaw and Strangeways West Junctions.

William Crompton died in 1892, he being the last surviving partner of the firm. In October 1897 the assets of Crompton & Shawcross were wound up as a result of a Chancery Court Judgement and the collieries, namely Strangeways Hall, Moss and Hindley (Edith and Mabel) Pits, were subsequently advertised for sale, along with

* See 'The Wigan Branch Railway' by the same author.

twelve miles of track, five locomotives, a five road repair shop, engine shed and 740 wagons. In the event, in October 1897 all were withdrawn from sale and in due course, acquired by J.E.Rayner on 20th December the same year, reopening under the title of Crompton & Shawcross Ltd.

The conglomeration led by principle shareholder Rayner, continued to purchase other collieries in the area, and having already purchased Hindley Field and Victoria Collieries prior to 1900, the Hindley Green Collieries of John Scowcroft were acquired in 1901.

Grange Colliery, Hindley, first appears in the mines list in 1901, under the occupation of Crompton & Shawcross Ltd., although originally, sinking had begun under the ownership of one John Hart. A branch line was built from Hindley & Platt Bridge Station to serve it, the connections provided by agreements of 1st June 1894 and 18th April 1899 between Hart and the Great Central Railway, endorsed by Crompton & Shawcross Ltd. on 20th May 1902. It is believed that the line did not open until after the new owners had acquired the colliery. The branch line would later be extended from Grange Colliery to the former John Scowcroft's Hindley Green mine, passing over the London & North Western's Tyldesley-Wigan line by an overbridge east of Scowcroft's Junction.

Grange Colliery was to close in 1927 but the sidings connections were not removed until 27th July 1938. Notations on the schedule says *Connected to L.U. line*, which it never was. With the number of collieries in this vicinity it's hardly surprising that someone made an error!

The Riding mine, although not physically connected to the Wigan Junction lines, also came into the ownership of J.E.Rayner in 1907, Crompton & Shawcross Ltd. taking over the agreements signed by the previous owner, one Henry Atherton. The colliery, however was short lived, closing in 1910, although the siding remained in use to serve a brickworks located on the site until 1914.

Likewise, Edith and Mabel pits were worked by Crompton & Shawcross from 1891 and later, J.E. Rayner who now had control of a number of collieries in the Amberswood and Hindley areas and had negotiated agreements with the London & North Western and Great Central Railway Companies. He could run his engines between Amberswood East & West Junctions over the Lancashire Union route thereby working from the Edith and Mabel pits to Strangeways Hall Colliery and, in respect of his arrangements with the Great Central, to reach his Grange, Hindley Green, Hindley Field and Victoria Collieries, thereby working over the Bickershaw Branch.

Plate 79. Stanier 2-6-4T No.42647 arrives at Hindley & Platt Bridge with a Wigan train on 31st October 1964. The all-timber buildings are typical of station construction along the route. *Peter Eckersley.*

Amberswood Colliery had been sunk by Richard Blundell in 1842 and was originally connected to the North Union lines at 600 yards south of Springs Branch. However, this connection was removed in the 1860s during the construction of the Wigan - Eccles Junction route. Another outlet was provided at Crompton's Sidings on the new route. On the death of Richard Blundell in 1853, the workings were taken over by his son, Henry, who, in the 1870s gave up the Amberswood mines. The Blundell name though will forever be associated with the Pemberton Collieries which remained in the family for over one hundred years.

The Ince Hall Coal & Cannel Company sank new shafts north of Blundell's Colliery, in the vicinity of Moss Hall Farm in June 1873. Blundell's railway was extended to serve it, but their coal was worked by Crompton & Shawcross, as part of the same area at Amberswood Common had also been leased to them. They had sunk collieries at Fir Tree House in 1864 and had taken over Strangeways Hall Colliery in 1875 laying a new line linking Strangeways Pits to their Fir tree House railway.

Having taken over Pearson & Knowles' Hindley Hall Colliery in 1904, Crompton & Shawcross Ltd. then constructed a new spur at Amberswood enabling traffic to reach Fir Tree House Sidings.

The Ince Hall & Cannel Company's pits at Amberswood had closed in the late 1880s, but had been reopened in 1894 by Crompton & Shawcross as Moss Colliery, a subsidiary of the company. The colliery railway which ran southwards, had been lifted after closure. It was relaid and a connection at Moss Colliery Sidings was instituted under an agreement with the Great Central Railway of 10th May 1894, coal traffic being dispatched as from 21st December 1896. The location is described on the agreement as: Moss Cutting Sidings, Moss Colliery (also known as Gypsy Pit).

The Private Sidings Schedule states that the colliery was closed in 1910 having been worked out, but was reopened on 30th October 1922 with an output of 50 tons per day, anticipated to be increased to 500 tons per day. In 1924 it was found to be working at a loss and closed permanently.

Plate 80. A nice array of the Railway Signalling Company's lower quadrant signals on the 'Down' platform at Hindley & Platt Bridge c1950 as viewed towards Amberswood. On the far side of the bridge (Liverpool Road) Amberswood East Curve comes in from East Junction. These signalling arrangements will date from the mid 1890s after a succession of line alterations on the North and South curves had been instituted, in particular to goods lines. *W.S.Garth.*

There may have been some intention on the part of the owners to work the coal from another direction, or even sink a new shaft, as it was not until 16th October 1934 that the sidings agreement was terminated, authorised by the LNER Divisional Manager, Crompton & Shawcross Ltd. paying £130 for removal of sidings and connections, completed by 3rd January 1935.

Plate 81. This view at Hindley South is looking towards Bickershaw where the London & North Western's lines built under the Hindley Junctions Railways Act can be seen in the right background running to Bickershaw. On 1st July 1964, 2-6-4T No.42631 departs from Hindley South with the 14.00 to Manchester Central. *Allan Heyes.*

Plate 82. It still says Hindley & Platt Bridge on the signal box c1951 but officially had changed to Hindley South on 1st July 1950. This view is looking north towards Amberswood Junctions and the Lancashire Union route, left for West Junction and Bamfurlong, right for East Junction and Standish. In the immediate foreground is Strangeways West Junction. By reference to *Figs 29 & 30,* it can be seen how the route to Wigan passes under the Lancashire Union. When the Wigan Junction Railways opened in 1879 it went only as far as Strangeways Hall Colliery and it would be some years before extensions to Darlington Street and, later still Wigan Central, were completed. *Jim Peden.*

Plate 84. This Wigan Junction Railways boundary stone at Hindley was, presumably, placed between the latter's railway and that of the London & North Western's Hindley Junctions lines south of the station. *John Marshall.*

Plate 83, top. Another view of Amberswood North Curve, this time from June 1962, taken from a passing train. The sidings into the goods yard, extreme right, appear to have been lifted and some signalling has been 'rationalized.
Eddie Bellass.

Plate 85. Hindley & Platt Bridge cabin having been re-named Hindley South has, evidently, recieved a much needed coat of paint. This photo also appears to be from the early 1960s and although the box itself seems to be in good order the encroaching vegetation is redolent of a railway in decline. The Lancashire Union route runs across the picture in the background. The signalman gazes in awe at the surrounding scenery.
Author's Collection.

Plate 86. an unidentified 2-6-4 tank engine passes through Hindley South Station in September 1964, signalled to take the Hindley Junctions line to Bickershaw Junction on the former London & North Western route. *Tom Sutch.*

Plate 87. Stanier 2-6-4T No.42607 running tender first approaches Hindley South with a service from Wigan Central on 18th August 1962. Liverpool Road bridge is in the background. The lines branch off to Amberswood East and West Junctions on the left and right respectively. This signal box here opened by 30th August 1936 replacing the original 1884 installation that had been built between the Up line and the Amberswood North Curve. *John Sloane Collection.*

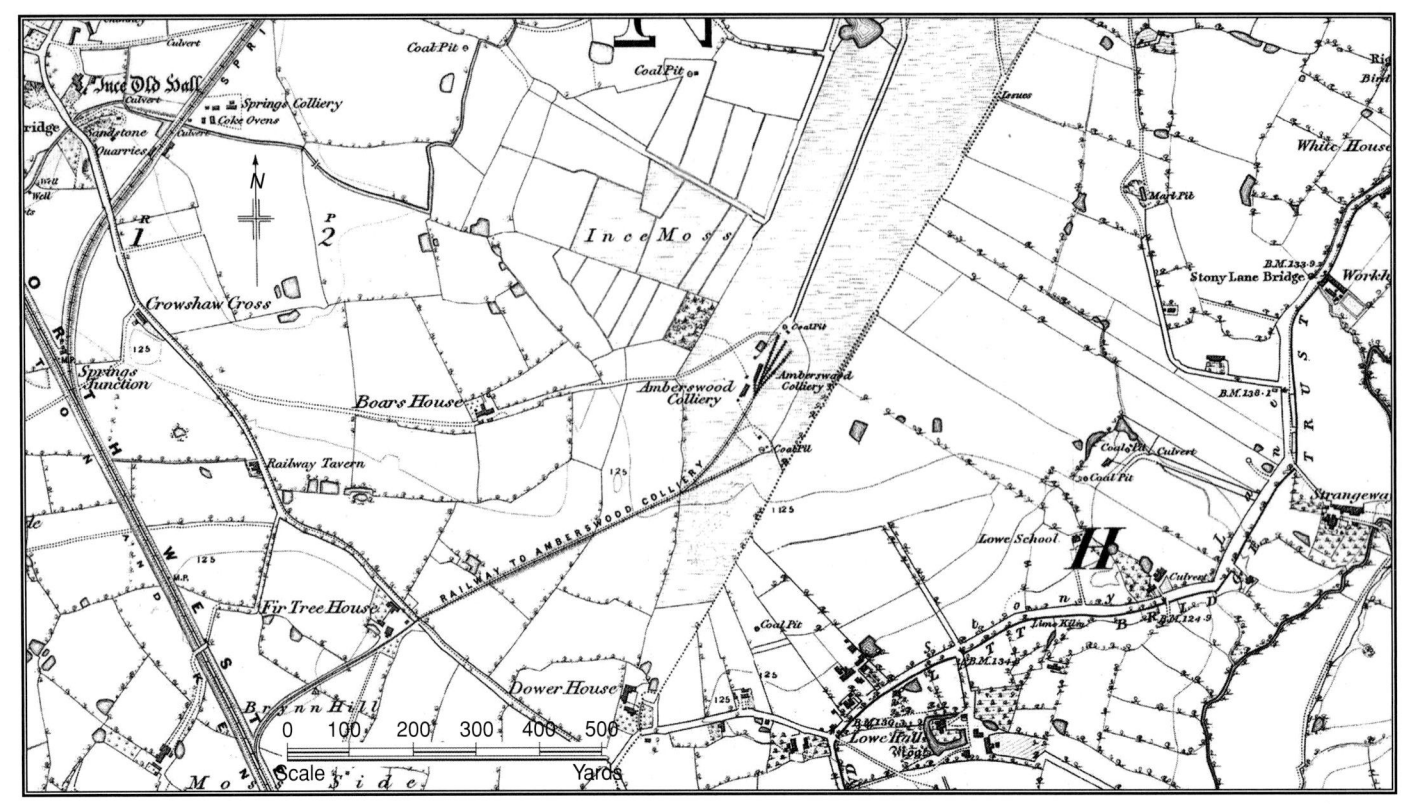

Fig 28. Amberswood Common c1849 and Amberswood Colliery which then had a connection with the North Union Railway some 600 yards south of Springs Branch. The colliery was opened by Richard Blundell in 1842 and after closure in the 1880s, reopened by Crompton & Shawcross in 1894. Compare this with *Fig 29* opposite, and note the incursions made by mines and railways over a period of 40 years.

Plate 88. With a mixture of ex L.N.E.R. and L.M.S. stock a Wigan Central - Manchester Central train approaches Hindley South in the early 1950s hauled by Stanier 2-6-4T No.42666. On the far right is Amberswood East Junction signal box. *Authors Collection.*

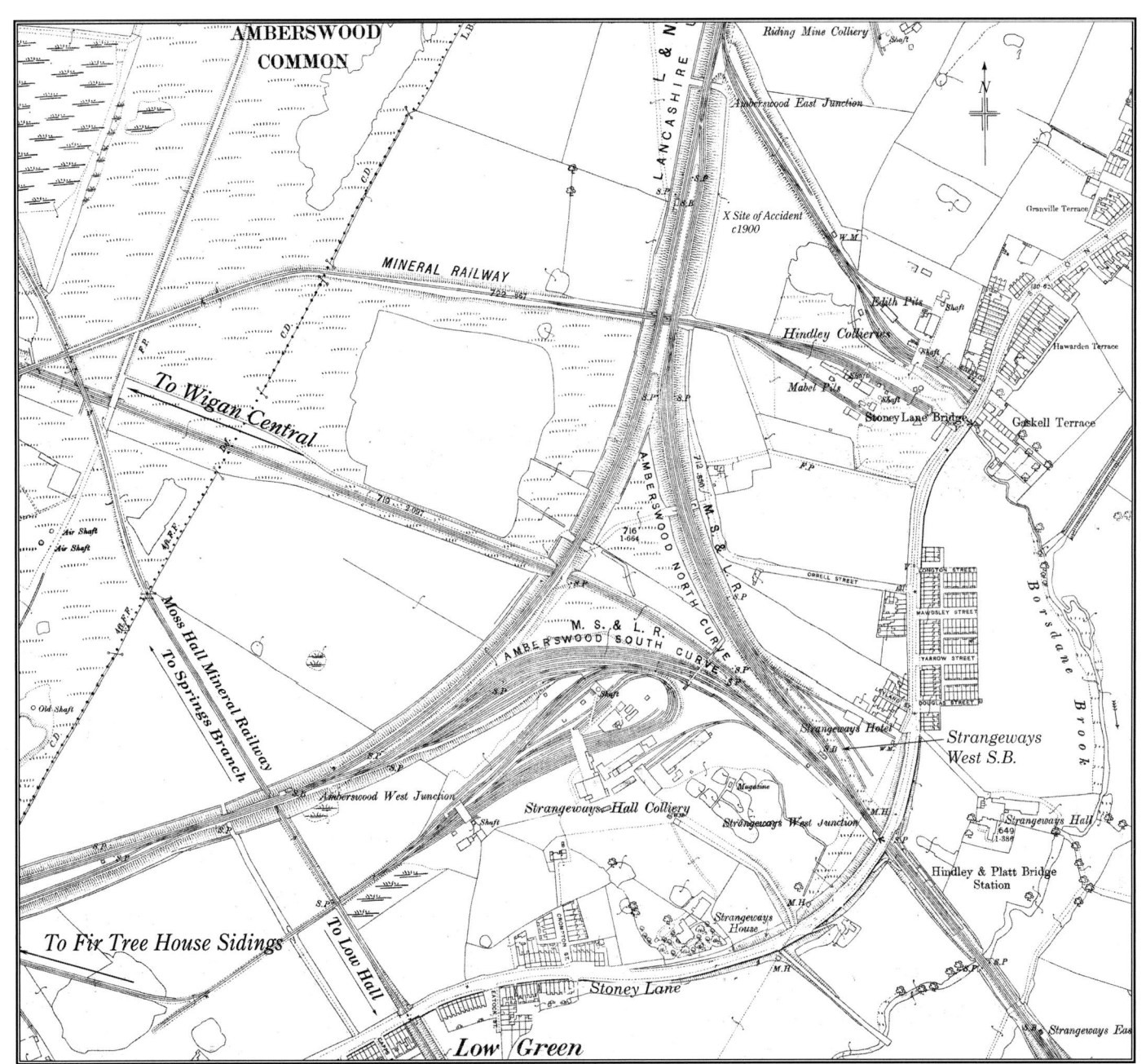

Fig 29. Strangeways Hall Colliery and Junctions at Amberswood from the second series Ordnance Survey c1888/1892. The colliery was hemmed in by Stoney Lane, (Liverpool Road, A58) the Lancashire Union lines and the Wigan Junction's lines. Amberswood South Curve, being on a much tighter radius than the north curve, left little room for sidings accommodation. Crompton & Shawcross linked Strangeways Hall Colliery to their railway at Fir Tree House in 1875, traffic accessing the London & North Western's Wigan lines at Crompton's Sidings. The Moss Hall Collieries Railway from Low Hall enters at bottom, left of centre, and continues to the Springs Branch. Engines of the Great Central and their decendents that were too large for the turntable at Wigan Goods Yard were turned on the Amberswood triangle. Under Great Central administration, Amberswood South and North Curves would be referred to as West and East Curves respectively. The positions of Strangeways East cabin of 1886 and West cabin of 1884 are seen, having Stevens and Railway Signal Co. boxes respectively, The first coal train departed from Strangeways Hall Colliery on the 17th October 1879. However, according to Nathaniel Eckersley in his address to those gathered at Mr R. Stone's residence when celebrating the opening of the railway, *the double line was not complete yet*. No indication was given though as to exactly which part. Strangeways West signal box is indicated, between the North Curve and the Up Main, having opened for the passengers service from Darlington Street in 1884 with 44 working levers. This is believed to have closed in August 1936 and a new box opened as seen in **Plates 82, 85 & 87**, sited alongside the Down line.

Plate 89. An unidentified ex-L&NW G2/A 0-8-0 passes the signal box on the Down line at Hindley South to make its way onto the curve towards Amberswood East Junction about 1963. In the background the Lancashire Union line runs across the picture, the lines to Wigan Central going under the bridge. On the left, in former times, was the connection into Strangeways Hall Colliery which had an operating life of almost a hundred years the last of the collieries closing in January 1937. The agreements regarding connections at Strangeways Hall and Grange Collieries was terminated as from 6th December 1938. Dirt tips like these here were dotted all over Wigan and the surrounding areas, and even in the 21st century have not totally been eradicated. *Eric Bentley.*

Hindley Hall Colliery first appears in the mines list in 1857, worked by Blackie & Knowles and, from 1859, by Pearson & Knowles, the lease being granted to John Pearson by John de Trafford on 1st May 1858. Pearson & Knowles constructed a private railway across Amberswood Moss to their Springs Colliery on the Springs Branch. Hindley Hall Colliery closed on 16th February 1904 and the colliery railway to Springs Branch lifted.

However, it appears to have been redeveloped before 1908 by Crompton & Shawcross Ltd., as it is shown on the updated Ordnance Survey of that year. The new owners relaid the colliery railway, which passed under the Lancashire Union's lines near Amberswood East Junction, but only as far as their Moss Colliery line where a new spur connecting the two private lines enabled the owners to work traffic either to Crompton's Sidings at Springs Branch or, via the new spur, by reversal, to Moss Cutting Sidings on the Wigan Junction Railways, now under Great Central ownership.

Operations at the colliery were suspended from 1917, re-opening after World War I before finally closing in 1921. The colliery railway running westward across Amberswood Moss was lifted, but part of the route from Moss Colliery, at its southern end, was retained as it served other companies, including the Strangeways Hall Colliery of Crompton & Shawcross Ltd.

On the main lines, the section between Hindley South and Lowton St. Mary's was last used for traffic on Saturday 2nd January 1965. For about two months afterwards the lines were used for the storage of empty vans which were shunted in from the Lowton end and at one time reached to Park Lane. The curve from Hindley South to Amberswood East Junction was taken o.o.u. on Monday 22nd February 1965 and the curve to Amberswood West Junction o.o.u. on Monday 8th March 1965*.

Hindley South signal box was closed and the line between Strangeways East Junction and Wigan singled and worked on 'one engine in steam' regulations for about 18 months.

The arrival at Hindley of the workmen's trains from Irlam was followed by a dash up the station steps to the trolley-bus stop on Liverpool Road, almost an enactment of 'the survival of the fittest' or the most cunning! The same enthusiasm not evident on the outward journey.

From information supplied by Tim Oldfield.

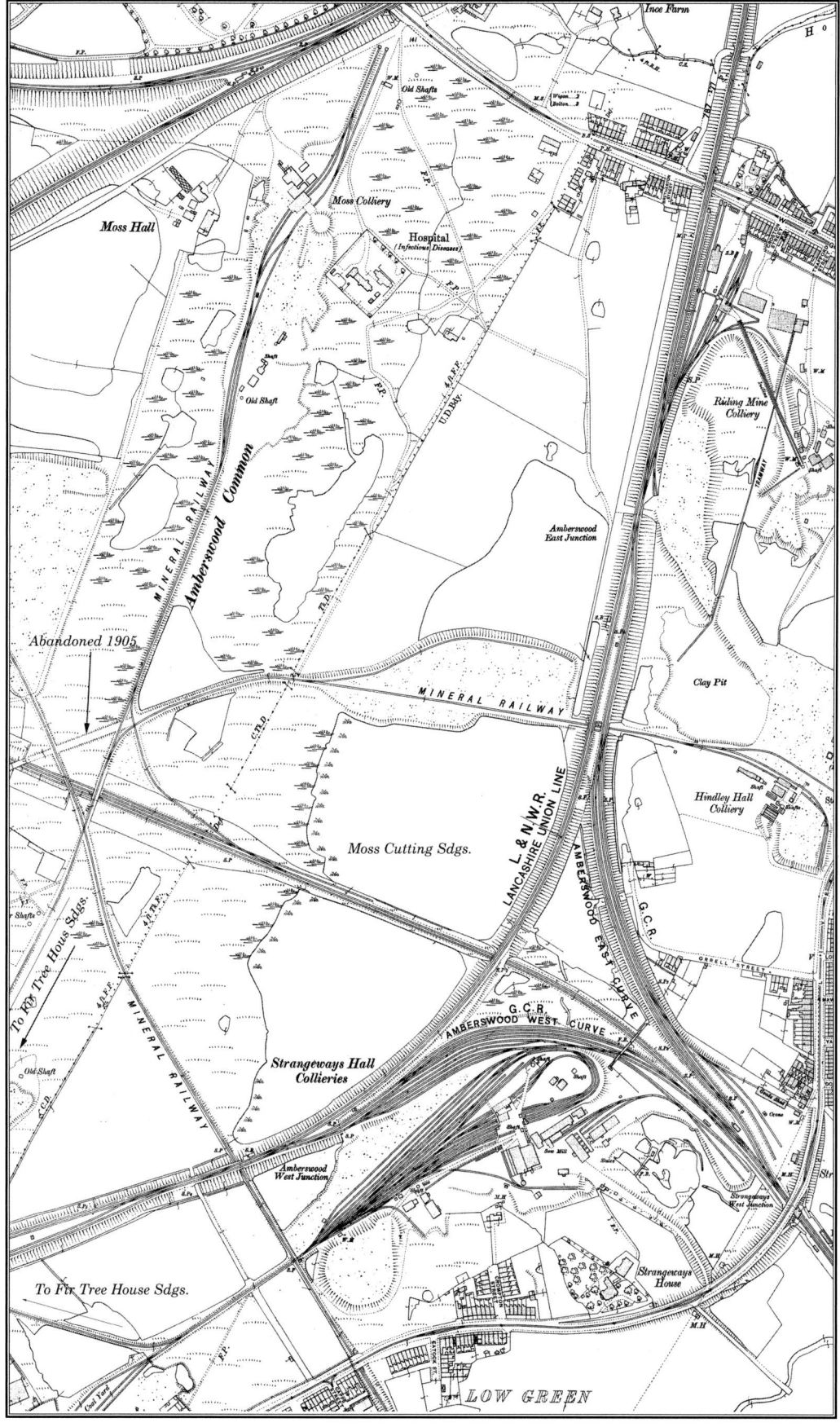

Fig 30. The 1907 revision shows some major changes to the railway infrastructure at Amberswood. The relaying of lines to serve the pits at Moss Colliery has taken place and a connection with the Wigan Junction Railways at Moss Cutting Sidings has been instituted. The former railway from the Hindley Hall Colliery of Pearson & Knowles to the Springs Branch has been lifted by the new owners, Crompton & Shawcross Ltd., west of their line to Moss Colliery, and now runs to Fir Tree House Sidings. At Strangeways Hall Colliery a new bank of sidings have been built between the pits and Amberswood West Curve. It will be noted that the nomenclature for the Amberswood curves has changed.

With improving freight traffic movements on the railway, between 1886 and 1896 successive changes had been made on the East & West Curves whereby through goods lines had been added or modified with the resultant signalling alterations.

It is worth noting at this point that the mining companies must have been making a fortune as the demand for coal had increased considerably over the years. However, the ones making the most were the landowners who were only too ready in allowing mining development to take place on their estates and, in the event could sit back and watch the money stack up, often many times than that originally anticipated without any financial risk whatsoever. It was the mine owners who took on the risk of sinking the shafts and winning the coal.

At the bottom of the hierarchy were the miners themselves who did all the grafting and suffering, hundreds dying in gas explosions or roof falls which would continue until the mining inspectors got to grips with the lax managerial practices at some of the collieries.

The Manchester, Sheffield & Lincolnshire Railway's New Works Act of 1881 were presented to Parliament in November 1880 and the following extracts are reproduced from the *Manchester Guardian* of 26th November inst.

A Railway No.2 commencing in the township of Hindley in the Parish of Wigan in the County of Lancaster, by a junction with Railway No.3 (Amberswood North Curve) authorised by the Wigan Junction Railways Act of 1874 at, or near, a point on that railway distant 1½ chains or thereabouts, measured in a northerly direction from the point where the said authorised Railway No.3 is intended to cross the colliery railway belonging, or reputed to belong to Pearson & Knowles Coal & Iron Company Ltd., and terminating in the Township of Ince-in-Makerfield, in the said Parish of Wigan, by a junction with the railway of the Wigan Coal & Iron Company Ltd., at a point on that railway distant 7 chains or thereabouts, measured in a southerly direction along that railway, from the point where that railway crosses the Bank House Brook. See **Fig 31** below.

A Railway No.3, wholly in the Township of Ince-in-Makerfield, in the Parish of Wigan, in the County of Lancaster, commencing by a junction with the Ince Hall Coal & Cannel Company's Railway, at a point on that railway under the centre of the bridge which carries Ince Green Lane over that railway, and terminating by a junction with the Liverpool, Bury & Manchester Branch of the Lancashire & Yorkshire Railway at a point on that railway 13 yards, or thereabouts, measured in an easterly direction along that railway from the centre of the bridge that carries that railway over Warrington Lane.

Railway No.3 was proposed to Make connections at Lower Ince with the Lancashire & Yorkshire Railway and the Ince Coal & Cannel Cos. Railway. *See plan* **Fig 32** *page 86 and Railway No.4 opposite.*

On 24th July 1900, a serious accident occurred near to Amberswood East Junction when a returning holiday special from Blackpool to Manchester derailed, killing the driver, one passenger and injuring twenty-five others, a full account of which will be found in *The Lancashire Union Railway* by the same author.

Although the Inspecting Officers report is ambiguous in its findings it appears that the track on the Wigan Junction's lines was, shall we say, substandard. This seems to be borne out by comments made by writer R.E.Charlwood in 1895 when he refers to very bad track through Hindley & Platt Bridge whilst making a journey on the 7.45am from Windermere to Manchester. A similar comment was made by a passenger from Manchester enroute to Windermere in the 1930s and, going by way of De Trafford Junction instead of Amberswood Junctions, escaping the unpleasant passage of the G.C.R.'s territory. *

Fig 31 left. The Manchester Sheffield & Lincolnshire Railway's New Works proposals of 1881 were contested by the London & North Western Railway and thus went before a Committee of Arbitration. Railway No.2 of the Act, a branch from Amberswood North Curve to the Wigan Coal & Iron Company's Railway north of the Lancashire & Yorkshire line was abandoned. Railway No.5, the short curve to the Springs Branch, already sanctioned by the 1874 Act upon which the earthworks were built but no track ever laid is shown as a dotted line. The Wigan Station as shown is Darlington Street, authorised under the 1881 New Works Act, the proposal for a station at Standishgate being withdrawn. *Courtesy, John Hall.*

* From the *Mancunian* c1984.

Courtesy, Peter Hampson.

LOWER INCE TO DARLINGTON STREET

A Railway No.4, wholly in the Township of Ince-in-Makerfield, in the Parish of Wigan, in the County of Lancaster, commencing by a junction with Railway No.3, at a point on that railway distant 12 yards, or thereabouts from the centre of the said Liverpool, Bury & Manchester Railway Branch of the Lancashire & Yorkshire Railway, measured at a right angle thereto in a southerly direction, and which said point on the Lancashire & Yorkshire Railway is distant 120 yards, or thereabouts, measured in a westerly direction along that railway over the Ince Hall Coal & Cannel Company's Railway, and terminating by a junction with the said Lancashire & Yorkshire Branch Railway at a point on that railway at or near the said last mentioned bridge, which intended railways, or some of them, will pass from, in, through or into the several parishes, townships, extra-parochial or other places following, namely, Wigan, Hindley, Atherton, Leigh, Westleigh, Abram and Ince-in-Makerfield, all in the County of Lancaster.

The above proposal for Railway No.4 was, without doubt, a most contentious issue by which the Wigan Junction Railways were attempting to squeeze in a connecting branch line to the Lower Works area and expecting the Lancashire & Yorkshire Railway to undergo an unbelievable amount of inconvenience, and probably interruption to their operations. There was insufficient space here and it beggars belief that the Wigan Company, or their masters, the Manchester Sheffield & Lincolnshire Railway, even tried it on. It was again a waste of planning resources and resultant costs. In the end there was barely enough room to get an engine shed here!

It was at Ince that the then Home Secretary, the Rt. Hon. R.A.Cross cut the first sod of the railway on 27th October 1876, watched by a crowd of onlookers and in his rather long-winded address spoke of the benefits it would bring to the locality and that the railway: *does not involve the erection of any elaborate or extensive engineering works, but from the nature of the district through which the line runs, there are several important bridges and no less than four lines of public railway being crossed by the new line.* At the later reception he goes on: *within a short distance were ten smelting furnaces, three large rolling mills and one forge. The coalfield through which the railway passed contained thirteen collieries producing 1 million tons annually and the line could easily and at a moderate cost be connected with seven other collieries producing two million tons annually. In addition to the collieries now at work, a new coalfield would be developed which was estimated to contain above 350 million tons.*

Plate 90. On 9th September 1988, a DMU is seen on the former Lancashire & Yorkshire lines at Lower Ince passing over the trackbed of the Wigan Junction Railways. Today, such has been the proliferation of unchecked vegetation, the bridge is all but obscured from view. This is the site of Lower Ince engine shed where, far left, a Kwik Save supermarket had been built, later demolished to make way for new housing. Beyond the bridge was the Lower Coal Works.
John Sloane.

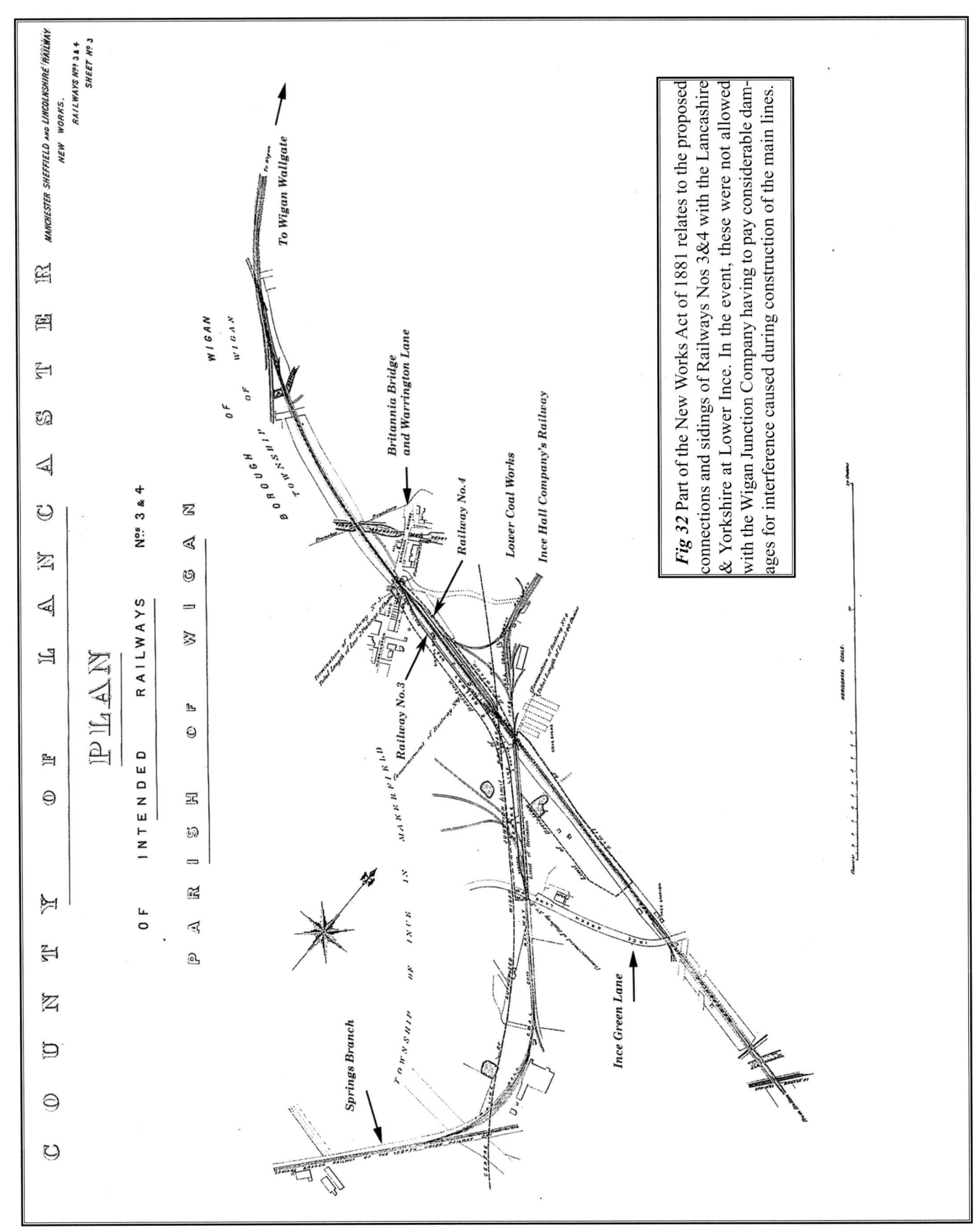

Fig 32 Part of the New Works Act of 1881 relates to the proposed connections and sidings of Railways Nos 3&4 with the Lancashire & Yorkshire at Lower Ince. In the event, these were not allowed with the Wigan Junction Company having to pay considerable damages for interference caused during construction of the main lines.

The area around Lower Ince once formed an intricate and complex part of the transport and mining infrastructure of this part of Wigan. Originally, the plans put forward by the Wigan Junction Railways' promoters in 1873 would have avoided this area entirely by building their station at Queen Street, but the objections of the London & North Western Railway soon put paid to that idea. It must have been with some trepidation therefore that the promoters realised they were being forced into a more easterly course in order to access Wigan.

However, the financial burden needed to overcome the engineering challenges of passing through Lower Ince was, fortunately for the Wigan Junction Railways, borne by the Manchester, Sheffield & Lincolnshire Railway, without whose assistance and money this railway would never have reached thus far and, it is extremely likely, that the London & North Western would have stepped in sooner or later with the end result being very different.

The insertion of the Wigan Junction Railways into Darlington Street was to be an expensive and torturous venture.

Major construction works had to be undertaken at Lower Ince and the burrowing bridge under the Lancashire & Yorkshire's Wigan Wallgate lines was yet another capital consuming construction which would bring the Wigan Company into the region of the Ince coalfield known as Lower Works. Contemporary references also give Bottom Place or Lower Place as alternative names for the location. It is an area through which the Leeds - Liverpool Canal cuts its way by a series of locks from Wigan Pier to Top Lock where it would join with the Lancaster Canal in 1816.

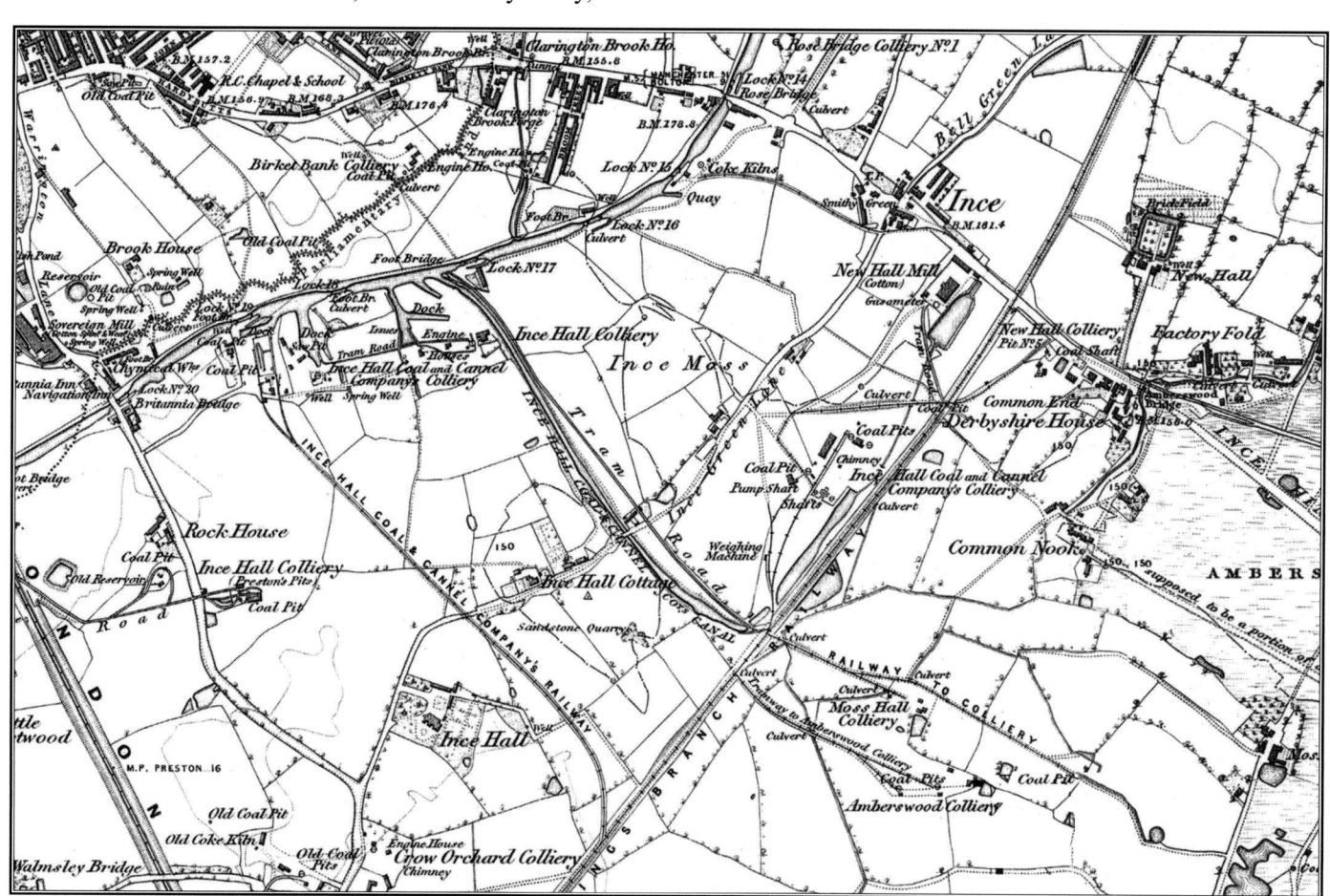

Fig 33. The area around Lower Ince is seen here as recorded on the mid 1840s Ordnance Survey. The Wigan Junction Railways as constructed would have to pass through this area and after passing under the Springs Branch ran parallel with the Ince Hall Coal & Cannel Company's Railway, the latter shown left of centre connecting to the Springs Branch. The next ordnance Survey would be in the late 1880s and, in the intervening period, more industry had been built alongside the Springs Branch, mining activity had increased and the Lancashire & Yorkshire's Railway to Wigan Wallgate had been constructed. It was far from being the ideal route for a new railway to be built at this late stage in the industrial development of Wigan.

N.B. The Amberswood Colliery shown near the Springs Branch is not that referred to on page 80.

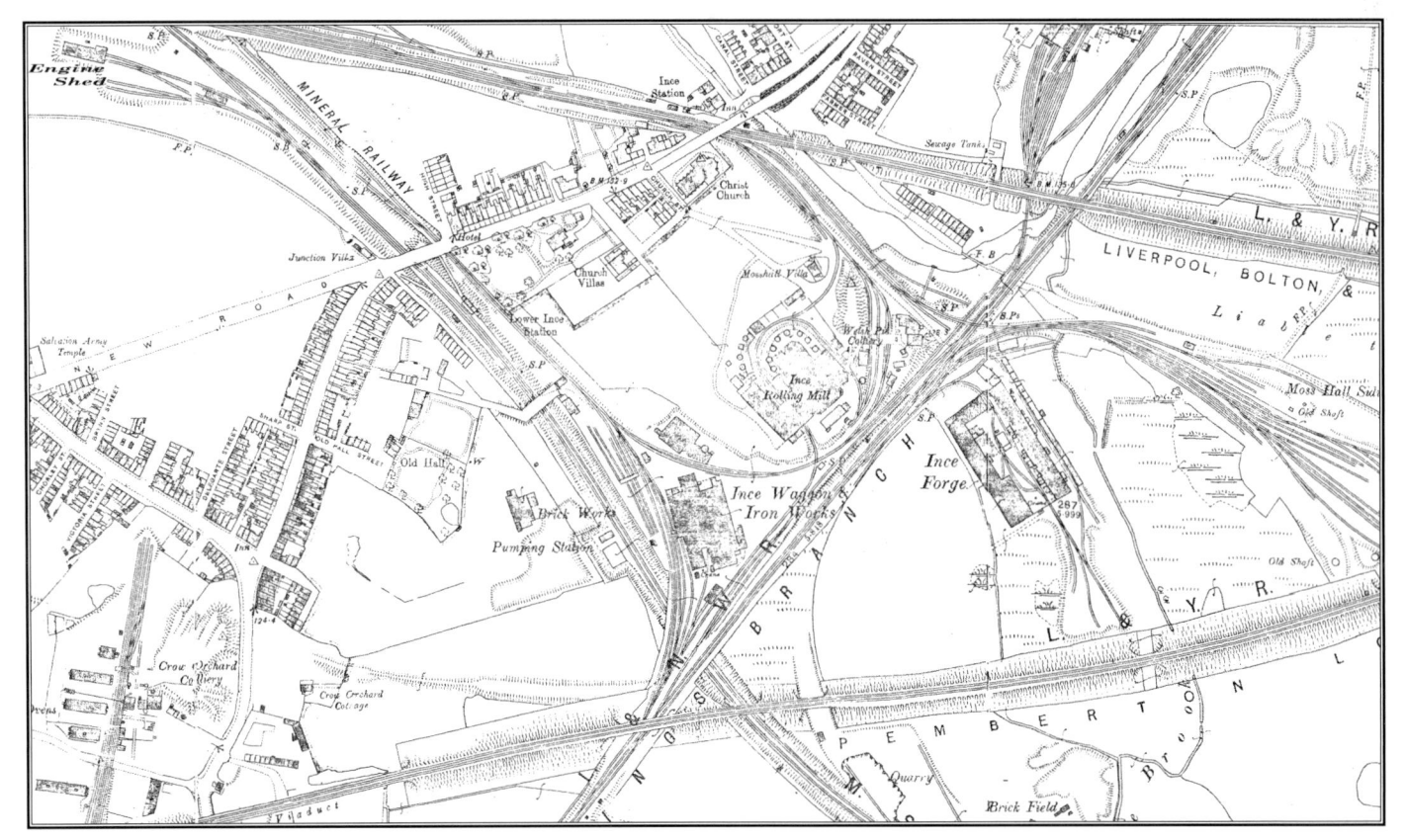

Fig 34. Lower Ince from the second series Ordnance Survey. The Wigan Junction Railways enter at bottom centre before passing under the Springs Branch and the connections of the Ince Hall Coal & Cannel Company to the latter. The Wigan Junction lines then run parallel with the Ince Hall Coal & Cannel's lines towards Lower Coal Works. Both the Ince Hall Cos., and the Wigan Junction lines pass under Ince Green Lane (shown as New Road here) and its extension to Warrington Road, namely Manley Lane. The Lancashire & Yorkshire's Ince Station is situated at top centre. Lower Ince Engine Shed is top left and the Lancashire & Yorkshire's line to Wigan Wallgate, opened in 1848, runs across the picture. Here a new underbridge would be constructed to take the Wigan Junction lines towards Darlington Street. Also of interest is the trackbed of the proposed connection to the Springs Branch, Railway No.5, authorised under the original Wigan Junction Railways Act of 1874. Railway 'C' of the 1875 Act, the branch to Parson's Meadow, would have begun 1 chain north of Ince Green Lane in the area occupied by Lower Ince Engine Shed.

The opening of this waterway was to galvanize the coal producers of Wigan to expand their enterprise along its banks with new mines, tramways and loading wharfs, often constructing new basins to facilitate the loading of barges.

As will be seen in *Fig 36,* page 97, the area known as the Lower Coal Works had more than its fair share of mines and transport infrastructure. By 1848, with the arrival of the Lancashire & Yorkshire route, Lower Works had been sandwiched between the latter and the canal. To fully appreciate what activity had taken place here we must go back to the 1820s.

R&T Swarbrick, in partnership with one James Berry, having obtained a lease for mining rights from Wm. Anderton, opened out a colliery below lock 17 near the canal and constructed a basin in 1823 near lock 18 which was not to be larger than 300 yards in length and 20 yards wide.

However, Swarbrick and Co. were soon in financial difficulties and their enterprise was mortgaged to one H. Nicholls in October 1826; other parts of the lease were transferred to George Caldwell and John Lord on 20th January 1830.

Caldwell already had mining interests at the Middle Works at Lower Ince and a tramway, believed to have been operating pre -1829, ran from a point near lock 17 to Moss Hall Colliery *(see Fig 33)* on the eastern side of the later Springs Branch which, after the Springs Branch opened in 1838, it would cross by a flat crossing allowing the transport of coal to the Leeds - Liverpool Canal from Moss Hall.

In 1832 Swarbrick and partners, or one of the new lessees, were opening up a new colliery at Lower Works and despite this new venture, or perhaps because of it, Swarbrick's financial troubles continued.

Continued on Page 96.

Plate 91. On 13th August 1966 the Wigan Area Railfans Society (WARS) ran a tour encompassing the lines of South Lancashire using Stanier 'Mogul' 2-6-0 No.42968 and a collection of brake vans. After working from Bickershaw Junction via Hindley South, the train is seen at Lower Ince enroute to Wigan Central. In the background is the Springs Branch and the curve into Ince Wagon Works and the Ince Hall Coal & Cannel Company's Railway to Lower Coal Works. In the background at a higher level is the former Lancashire & Yorkshire's Pemberton Loop line which ran from Hindley to Pemberton Junction enabling express trains working from Manchester Victoria to Liverpool Exchange to by-pass Wigan Wallgate. The bridge in the background, under which the train has just emerged, had abutments which were 212ft in length, supporting 37 girders which carried the Springs Branch and its associated lines and connections over the Wigan Junction route. The building to the right of the train contained two centrifugal pumps to carry away the drainage from the Wigan lines into a purpose built reservoir which then drained into Ince Brook. With bridge and engineering works like these, it's no wonder the Wigan Junction Railways cost a fortune to build. *Tom Heavyside.*

Plate 92. The Manley Hotel, adjacent to bridge 44, is seen here about 1950 and is now a doctor's surgery. The bridge has been swept away and the area landscaped. The extant, former Lancashire & Yorkshire's Ince Station is but a few yards up the road. *B.R.*

Fig 35. One Peter Ashcroft, worked a quarry alongside the up line at Lower Ince, near to the Lancashire & Yorkshire Railway overbridge which carried their Pemberton Loop lines. The date of the original agreement to work this quarry is unknown but in 1901, a further Agreement with the Great Central authorised the letting of 5 acres of land bordering the two railways for a period of 21 years. The Railway Company were to construct a new sidings connection from the up main line approximately 80 yards in length, together with a new cross-over to the down line. It is presumed that Ashcroft would amend his internal sidings to suit his working arrangements.

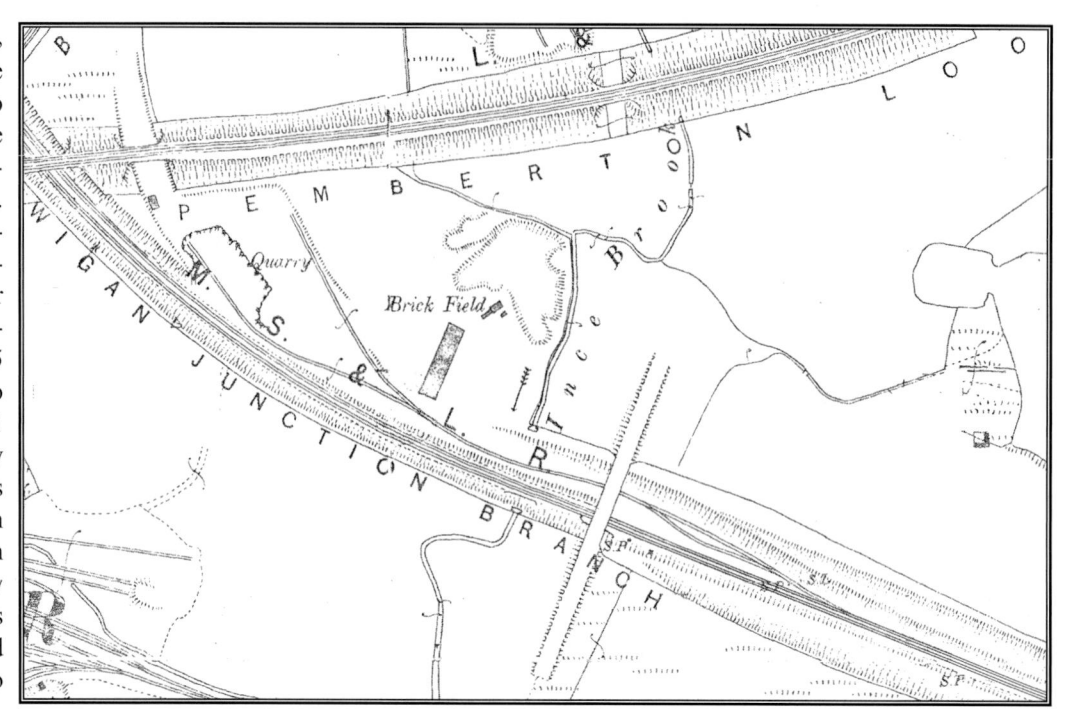

The original connection is shown here from the second series Ordnance Survey. It appears that the quarry as worked at this period was on the trackbed of the uncompleted spur to the Springs Branch. This, as already said, was a part of the Wigan Junction Railways Act of 1874, Railway No.5, amended in 1875 after the company were refused permission to build their station in Queen Street. Railway No.1 of the 1874 Act would have deviated towards Queen Street from this area. Railway 'A' of the 1875 Act, which included the resited station at Standishgate, would have begun six chains north of the Lancashire Union overbridge at Amberswood but shows little deviation towards Ince.

Plate 93. This view of Lower Ince dates from 1917, showing the housing on Junction Terrace which can also be seen in Peter Eckersley's photo opposite.
Cliff Reeves.

Plate 94. The view southwards over Bridge 44 at Ince Green Lane in the early 1950s. Lower Ince Station was situated on the left, that is, South-East of the bridge. The notice board contains details of fares to Goole and Hull amongst other places formerly served by the Great Central Railway.
B.R.

Plate 95. Stanier 2-6-4T No.42570 pauses at Lower Ince on 25th October 1964 with a Manchester Central service. There appears to be some custom for the train albeit ever so minimal.
Peter Eckersley.

Plate 96. Viewed in the opposite direction to *Plate 95*, is the desolated scene at Lower Ince Station after closure. Overlooked by Junction Terrace on the right, the sidings on the extreme left are filled with condemned wagons waiting for scrapping by Central Wagon Co., This is part of the railway first laid by James King & Co./Ince Hall Coal & Cannel Co. about 1843 from their mines near lock 19 at Lower Works, to the Springs Branch.

Bill Yates.

Plate 97. A view from the end of Lower Ince 'Up' platform of the water tank at Lower Ince Shed. Note the bridge girder makers inscription ' DALLAM FORGE WARRINGTON 1881' and the effects of mining subsidence on the right-hand abutment. *B.R.*

LOWER INCE SHED

Plate 98. Lower Ince Shed was built in an area bounded by the Lancashire & Yorkshire lines and Warrington Road. In this view, c1962, a Wigan bound train approaches Lower Ince signal box, another of the Railway Signal Co's. installations, which was sited opposite the shed access junction. In all probability the box would have been inspected on 9th February 1884 in preparation for the beginning of passenger services. In the background the former Lancashire & Yorkshire route crosses the lines to Wigan Central.
Eddie Bellass.

Plate 99. The photographer quickly moves across to the other side of the coach and photographs the delapidated scene of Lower Ince. The shed had closed on 26th March 1952 and a number of Class 'J10' locomotives transferred to Springs Branch Shed to work the early morning workmen's services to Irlam and general passenger turns until eventually replaced by ex-LMS designs. A number of footplate staff were also transferred to Springs Branch, others to Trafford Park Shed.
Eddie Bellass.

Plate 100. Class 'J10s' Nos.5080 & 5837 are seen at Lower Ince Shed in 1937. In the early 1940s a number of 'J10s' were noted on shed here, a mixture from the pre- and post-Thompson renumbering scheme.:- Nos.5077, 5080, 5121, 5122, 5132, 5159, 5162, 5170, 5203, 5678, 5815, 5817, 5832, 5836, & 5848.
Author's Collection.

Plate 101. A rare photograph at Lower Ince Shed on 22nd June 1933 of 0-6-0 Class 'J69' No.7371 and 0-6-2 Class 'N5' No.5537. These two locomotives were later transferred away, 5537 only a month after on 7th July, whilst 7371 remained at Lower Ince until 14th April 1934, being moved to Trafford Park Shed.
John Sloane Collection, A.C.Roberts.

Plate 102. Lower Ince Shed is seen after closure. The siding on the right is the East Street Coal Depot as instituted for use by Crompton & Shawcross by an agreement with the Great Central Railway in 1904.
Author's Collection.

Plate 103. A nicely posed view of Class 'J10' No.5812 at Lower Ince Shed in June 1937. At nationalisation in 1948 it would be renumbered to 65148.
John Sloane Collection, (W.L.Good).

Plate 104. One of the Sacre designed 0-6-0 double-framed Class 'J12s' No.6434 on Lower Ince Shed about 1924.

A number of 'J12s' were shedded at Lower Ince in the 1920s but gradually these were replaced by 'J10s'. The first to arrive in 1927 was No.5812 transferred from Stockport and this class became the mainstay of services for both freight and passenger workings until the early 1950s when ex LMS types began to make inroads into the services, in particular the Stanier 2-6-4 tanks which, with their nippy acceleration, were well suited to branch line workings. *John Sloane Collection.*

Plate 105. 'Sentinel' Railcar No.51915 at Lower Ince on 19th May 1935. Four of these railcars were purchased in 1929 and during W.W.II, worked only intermittently. The first of these 'Sentinels,' No.51908 *Expedition* arrived at Lower Ince on transfer from Lowestoft. No.51912 *Rising Sun* stood in for 51908 between 27th June 1932 to 8th August 1932, whilst the latter received works attention. No.51914 *Royal Forrester* replaced 51908 in April 1933 until itself replaced by 51915 which was transferred from Gorton on 6th July 1934. It appears these railcars did not work on Saturdays and did not work into Manchester, their usual limit being Wigan to Partington on workmen's services, and to Irlam on Sundays. However, they also worked the St. Helens Branch occasionally. After a period of storage at Trafford Park Shed they were sent to Doncaster for scrapping in 1944. *John Sloane Collection (G.Coltas).*

A letter from John Lord to the landowner, Wm. Anderton in 1835, notes that Swarbrick is still in arrears with his rent but advised against foreclosure as this could result in other mines being flooded which seems to indicate that there was a pumping engine at one of Swarbrick's mines.

Richard Swarbrick retired from the partnership on 5th February 1838, leaving the then partners, Thomas Swarbrick and T.G.Bennet in partnership as T.G.Bennet & Co. However, shortly afterwards they withdrew from the mining business and their lease was taken up by other colliery owners.

Part of the Swarbrick leases had been taken over by James Whalley and F.Gerard on 22nd April 1835 and it is believed it was they who sank new pits near to Swarbrick's older workings as, on 17th February 1837, Whalley and Gerard were authorised to construct another canal basin between lock 17 and 18 and it is known they took over the basin constructed by Swarbrick in 1823.

On the scene now comes John Lancaster who already had mining interests at Patricroft and now turned his attention to the Wigan area. On 12th May 1843, having entered into a partnership with James Hodgkinson and James King, obtained a lease from Wm. Anderton for mining rights in the area previously leased to Richard Swarbrick.

Plate 106. Darlington Street is seen about 1920, upper right, when in use as a goods yard and at bottom right is Lower Ince Shed and the coal sidings alongside East Street. Wigan North Western Station is at top left. The complete absence of road traffic on Warrington Road centre, save for one vehicle, possibly a tram, is apparent. The road seen between the Lancashire & Yorkshire and the Wigan Junction lines that exits on Warrington Lane is that referred to in the text, re-the agreement of 29th December 1880. *Author's Collection.*

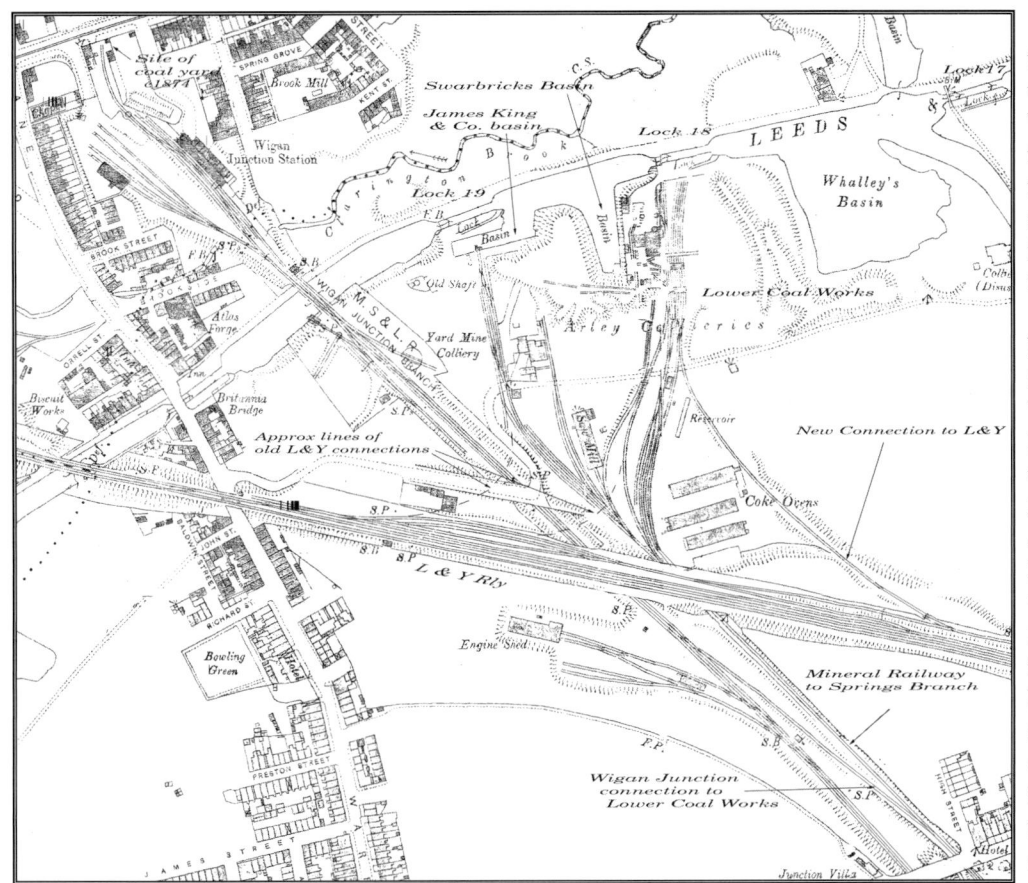

Fig 36. Darlington Street is seen in this Ordnance Survey from 1888 when in use as the terminus of the Wigan Junction Railway. There are two goods sheds and it is presumed that the larger one is in use for passenger trains as this would give easier access along Brook House Street.

As can be seen, there are a number of connections to coal pits here from the area known as Lower Coal Works. Whalley's Basin is top right. In the centre are 'Arley Collieries' which in fact are the mines sunk by James King & Co. reaching the Arley seam at a depth in excess of 300 yards and otherwise Known as 'Patricroft Mines' on account of John Lancaster originating from there. Yard mine is thought to have been worked by J.Marsden who had a lease of 21 years from 1888, and also for Alliance Colliery north of Crompton St. At top left is where the coal yard had been sited in 1874 on Darlington Street.

Known as James King & Company or the Ince Hall Coal & Cannel Company, they sank two new pits adjacent to lock 19 on the Leeds - Liverpool Canal and constructed a new private railway from these mines to connect with the Springs Branch, all of which appear on the 1st edition of the Ordnance Survey c1845/9. They were also given permission to construct a new basin above lock 19.

On 1st January 1847, John Swindells & Company, of which John Lancaster's brother, William, was a partner, took over James King & Co's. collieries adjacent to lock 19. It became known as Lower Patricroft Colliery but was also known as the Arley Pits. Swindells' other mining concerns were at the Middle Coal Works, alongside the Springs Branch. On 8th January 1848, a joint stock company was formed entitled, The Ince Hall Coal and Cannel Company which took over the operation of their collieries at both Lower Coal and Middle Coal Works.

We are now at the period when the Lancashire & Yorkshire Railway were about to open their line to Wallgate on 20th November 1848. Having originally been the Manchester & Southport Railway, it had been leased to the Lancashire & Yorkshire Railway prior to the former's opening on 5th May 1848.

At the Lower Coal Works, two west facing spurs had been built to connect the Ince Hall Coal & Cannel Co's. mines with the new main line which offered the colliery the luxury of sending out their coals either by canal, the Springs Branch or the Lancashire & Yorkshire route. About 1874 the Ince Hall Co. opened a landsales yard at Darlington Street which was connected by a tramway from Lower Works, originating near lock 19. The 1876 Wigan Town Plan shows this tramroad crossing Clarington Brook and the Leeds-Liverpool Canal.

It is against all this industry that the Wigan Junction Railways had to contend when construction began. No wonder it cost the paymaster, the Manchester Sheffield & Lincolnshire Railway, a fortune.

It had been the intention of the Wigan Junction Railways to construct two spurs connecting with the Lancashire & Yorkshire lines at Lower Ince to syphon off some of the coal traffic from Lower Coal Works. However, the relevant Act did not allow this.*

Section 33 of the Wigan Junction Railway Act of 1875 required that the Ince Hall Coal & Cannel Cos. connection with the Lancashire & Yorkshire must be maintained and in the event, this was moved closer to Ince Station because of the required bridge work to be carried out here.

*See pages 85-87

It appears that the Wigan Junction Railways had constructed their railway over land leased for a period of 999 years to the Ince Hall Coal & Cannel Company at Lower Coal Works, upon which a cart road connected Lower Works with Warrington Road. It also appears the coal company had sidings upon railway land. I take these to be the east to north facing connections to the Lancashire & Yorkshire lines east of Warrington Road. *(Shown as 'old connections' in **Fig 36**)*.

Under an agreement of 29th December 1880, between the Coal Co. and the Wigan Junction Railways, the latter were to build a bridge to carry the cart road over their railway and to pay the Ince Hall Coal & Cannel Company £350 to remove the latter's sidings. The same agreement notes that the Ince Hall Coal & Cannel Company's leasehold of the coal yard at Darlington Street was purchased by the Wigan Junction Company for the sum of £50. Neither the tramway that served it, nor the coal yard appear on subsequent O/S updates.

Further expense for the Wigan Junction Railways was to follow as, by an Agreement of 11th May 1881, they were to pay £15,000 to the Ince Hall Coal & Cannel Company on account of interference with the coal company's connections with the Lancashire & Yorkshire Railway

Therefore, the connection to Lower Coal Works materialised as a link from the Ince Hall Coal Company's lines north of Lower Ince Station, to the Wigan Junction Lines near Lower Ince Shed, just south of the new overbridge carrying the Lancashire & Yorkshire lines.

This was not quite the end of events at Lower Coal Works though. The Ince Hall Coal & Cannel Company had become a limited concern on 10th May 1871, prospering until declared bankrupt in 1884. In August of 1885 the Arley mines were reopened by Crompton & Shawcross who continued to use the rail connections of the former owners.

By the publication of the updated O/S in 1907 most of the sidings here and the connection to the Lancashire & Yorkshire line had disappeared, only the colliery line built by James King & Co. in the 1840s to the Springs Branch surviving.

The Arley Mines, as taken over by Crompton & Shawcross which in their ownership were referred to as Ince Hall Arley Pits, closed in 1892 and were subsequently dismantled. On 13th October 1892, a sale of plant and equipment included an 0-6-0 engine with 11in x 22in cylinders. However, to maintain coal deliveries to Higher Ince, Crompton & Shawcross Ltd., (J.E.Rayner) opened a new landsales depot in the goods yard at 'Lower Ince Station' under an agreement of 4th October 1904, whereby coal was conveyed by special rates from Victoria, Grange and Strangeways Hall Collieries.

In fact, the yard was at the end of East Street, off Warrington Road, the sidings alongside Lower Ince Shed having been extended under the 1904 Act, constructed and maintained by the Railway Company, for use by Crompton & Shawcross for the sale of coal.

The area was enclosed, and a gated entrance on East Street was provided. Item 3 of the agreement stipulated that :- *Upon completion of the siding the Traders shall be at liberty to use the land for the purposes of a depot for the sale of coal and the Traders shall keep the gate leading to East Street locked at all times when the land is not in use and indemnify the Railway Co. against trespass.*

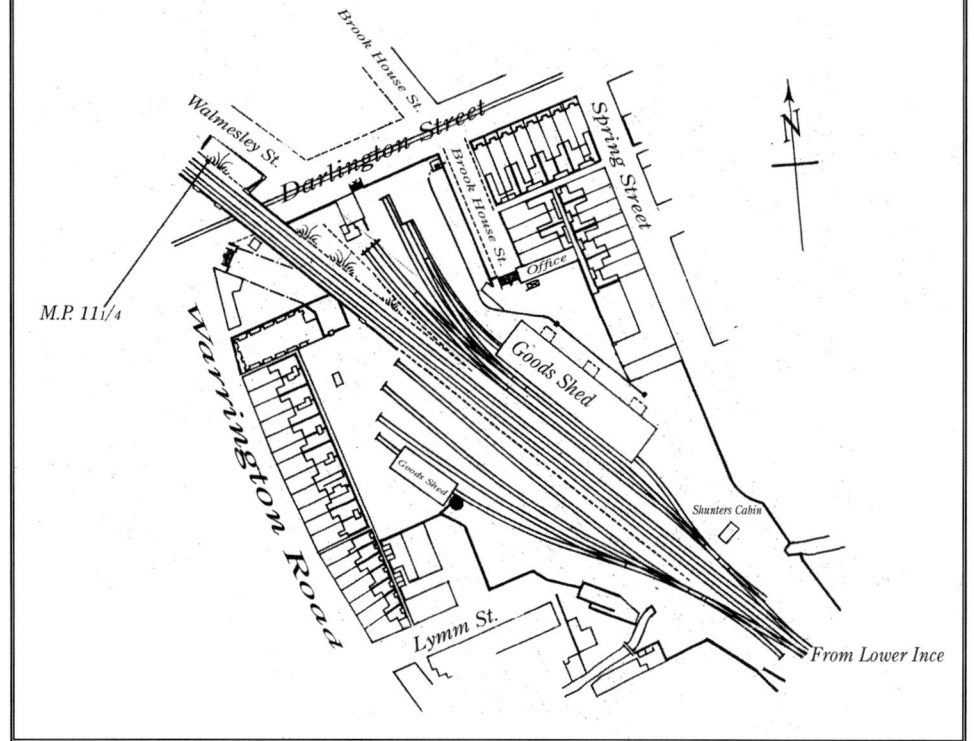

Fig 37. Darlington Street in late Great Central days. The lines continuing into Wigan Central begin at far right.

Lancashire Associated Collieries, formed on 1st July 1935, took over the yard as from 1st July 1939, underwriting the previous agreement on 28th June 1940.

However, after nationalisation of the mines on 1st January 1947 the new owners, the National Coal Board, terminated the 1904 and 1940 agreements as from 31st March 1948.

Ince Railway Wagon Works came into being in the 1850s. It is certainly not shown on the first series Ordnance Survey of the mid 1840s. It is shown in the ownership of one Richard Preston in 1858 who died about 1870/1.

Olive & Sons are believed to have taken over the works shortly afterwards, as a note in the Sidings Schedule dated 1st December 1878, states that Olive's Works was reached over the private railway of the Ince Hall Coal & Cannel Company's railway off the Springs Branch. Furthermore, it seems that the Ince Hall Co's. railway provided an outlet to the Wigan Junction Railways at Lower Ince for Olive & Sons and it seems likely that Ince Hall Coal & Cannel Co. worked the latter's traffic and did any shunting required.

By 1881, Olive & Sons were bankrupt and their works was taken over by the Ince Waggon & Ironworks Company Ltd., formed on 12th February 1883.

After the demise of the Ince Hall Coal & Cannel Company in 1884, their railway, and their mines at Lower Works were worked by Crompton & Shawcross.

Following the abandonment of the pits at Lower Works by Crompton & Shawcross in 1892, the Ince Waggon & Ironworks Co. Ltd., took over the railway from its junction with the Springs Branch, not only to maintain a connection with the Wigan Junction Railways, but also to reach the coke ovens built in the 1870s at Lower Works.

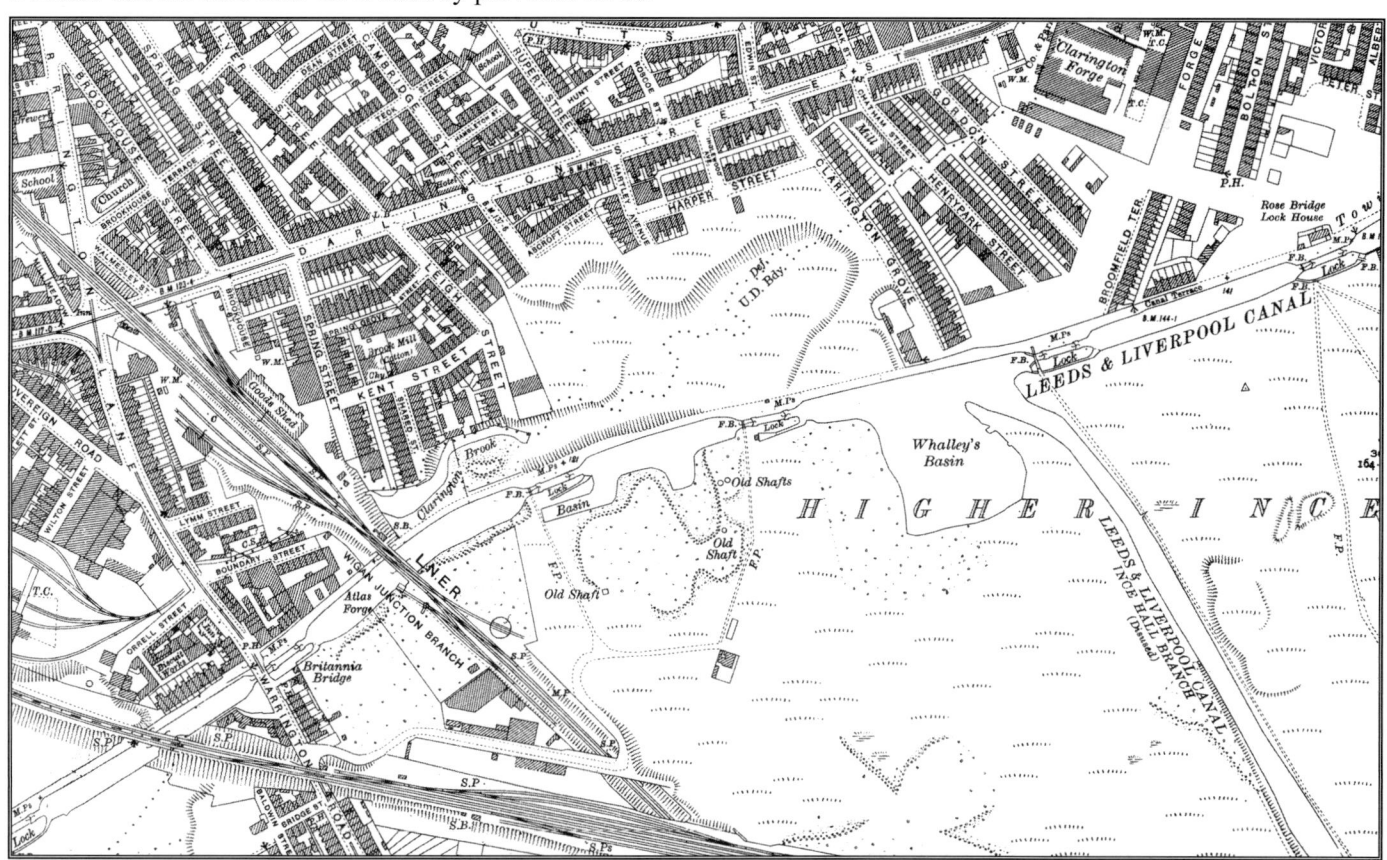

Fig 38. Lower Coal Works and Darlington Street Goods Yard from a mid 1920s updated Ordnance Survey. By this date all the mining activity at Lower Coal Works had ceased and the railways to it lifted and the area left bare. Even to this day no construction work has taken place here; it has in fact, returned to nature with the odd footpath linked by a bridge over the canal. Some house building has taken place on the opposite side of the canal where the bare area is shown and some of the older properties demolished. The former Ince Hall Coal & Cannel Company's canal branch, far right, is thought to have been filled in by the time this edition was printed.

Note the position of the turntable which is within sight of the signal box, the latter sited on the north side of the canal bank. It was about this period that single line working into Wigan Central began and the token collected from this box.

Part of the former Ince Hall & Cannel Co's line from Lower Works was purchased by the Wigan Junction Railways under an agreement of 20th Sept 1894 for £31.13s.7d. (£31. 68p) A further agreement of 17th Jan 1898 with the Great Central and Ince Waggon & Ironworks seems to confirm this.

The works was taken over by one W.R.Davies in 1919, unfortunately not with any degree of success, as closure occurred in 1932. It was to become a part of Central Wagon Company Ltd. in 1933, although continuing to trade under its old name.

A new agreement with the London & North Eastern was made on 25th Dec 1943 in respect of the sidings connection at Lower Ince, which in effect cancelled the 1898 agreement. An agreement with the recently formed British Transport Commission on 22nd March 1948, permitted the traders to use certain sidings and to maintain them at their own cost to the satisfaction of B.R.'s Engineer and that the *Commission shall only receive and deliver to 'Point x' and shall not be called upon to do any shunting.*

Plate 107. On 31st August 1964 Type '2' diesel No.D7586 crosses the Leeds-Liverpool Canal bridge working the 09.00 to Manchester Central. The redundant turntable and Wigan Goods signal box are seen, as is the large goods shed, extreme right. Wigan Goods Yard signal box opened on 9th February 1884 for the beginning of the passenger services. However, some alterations to the box were carried out by the Railway Signalling Company by 4th November 1885. The box is shown on the north side of the Leeds-Liverpool Canal in *Figs 36 & 38*. *Allan Heyes.*

Plate 108. The entrance into Darlington Street goods yard from the latter's junction with Warrington Lane is seen about 1971. *Bill Yates.*

Plate 110, opposite. Great Central signalling at Wigan Goods Yard c1964. It is believed that in 1925 traffic to Wigan Central Station became single line working, the token being obtained from Wigan Goods Yard box. This box was to close on 10th May 1966. *Allan Heyes.*

Plate 109. The bridge which carried the railway enroute to Wigan Central Station crossed, first, Darlington Street as seen above, and continued across Warrington Lane. This view on 29th July 1967 looks along Darlington Street towards Ince with a nice collection of vehicles; a Ford Zodiac has a green light to proceed with Mini and a Reliant Robin approaching. On the corner a Ford Consul is parked.
Allan Heyes.

Plate 111. A recent view south towards Britannia Bridge and lock 20 from lock 19 is in stark contrast to the former industrialisation of the area at Lower Coal Works. The Wigan Juction Railway crossed the Leeds-Liverpool Canal here just beyond the fencing, seen mid-picture, right.
Author.

When passenger services began in 1884, two sets of coaches would be required, one based overnight at Darlington Street, and one at Manchester Central. Later, when the main service operated from St. Helens, two sets were stabled at Manchester, one at St. Helens and a further set at Wigan for the local service to Lowton St. Mary's.

It is believed that these services in the early years of the railway were worked by engines from Cornbrook Shed.

In 1886, five freight trains departed from Darlington Street; an 8.15am to Northwich, a 4.40pm departure to Widnes and a 7.0pm train for Heaton Mersey, the other two went only to Glazebrook. Balanced workings ran in the opposite direction. By 1910 there were additional freight trains to Bidston, Halewood and Ashburys.

After W.W.I., all the direct trains to Manchester ran from St. Helens at 8.13am, 10.00am, 2.08am, 5.00pm and 9.00pm, with four return services at 8.00am, 12.33pm, 3.33pm and 7.33pm. Two other trains ran, the 6.40am from Tiviot Dale to St. Helens and the 5.40pm Lowton St. Mary's, the latter connecting with the 5.40pm Glazebrook-Wigan Central. During this same period nine trains ran between Wigan Central and Glazebrook, plus an extra two on Saturdays which only ran to Lowton. One of these only ran from Westleigh & Bedford to Lowton. Most, if not all of these rosters, would have been worked by a 'J12' from Lower Ince.

For a number of years in the 1920s a push-pull set was based at Wigan for working the Lowton service and Wigan return, the same set also working the 6.35am Wigan Central - Partington service and an evening train to St. Helens. A second set kept at Wigan, consisting of two brake thirds, two thirds and a brake composite, worked the workmen's trains to Westleigh & Bedford. On Saturdays this worked the 11.35 Wigan - Glazebrook and return service.

Except for a brief period during the 1926 miner's strike when a reduction in the number or workings occurred, the services generally followed the pattern as mentioned with, in the 1930s, a Sunday service being introduced with five trains between Wigan and Irlam, but none on the St. Helens branch. The operation of these services to Irlam is probably concomitant with the closure of Kirkless Iron & Steel works and the opening of the facilities at Irlam, to where many of the Kirkless workers were transferred.

After W.W.II., there were nine passenger trains from Wigan (eleven on Saturdays) comprising four to Irlam (five on Saturdays) two for Manchester Central and one each to Partington and Glazebrook. Six trains departed St. Helens, three to Manchester, two to Lowton and one to Partington with an extra train to Lowton on Saturdays. In the opposite direction, five trains ran to St. Helens and twelve to Wigan.

Apart from the Workmen's trains to Risley there were still unadvertised trains to Irlam and Manchester Central. By 1948 though, a miserable four trains per day served the St. Helens line.

In the early 1950s 'J10s' still had the lion's share of passenger workings to St. Helens and Wigan but the ex-LMS types, Ivatt 2-6-0s and Stanier/Fairburn 2-6-4 tanks, steadily made their appearance in ever increasing numbers. Lower Ince Shed had closed on 24th March 1952 and the remaining stud of 'J10s' transferred to Springs Branch and these continued to work the early workmen's services to Irlam for a while.

Come the 1960s, BR Standard class '4s' and Stanier Class '5s' made an appearance and, occasionally, type '2' diesels, later to become class '25s'.

Plate 112. The former site of Darlington Street station and goods yard is seen in November 2012. The road is Kingscroft Court, the first construction on the site was the red-bricked office building on the left.
Author.

Plate 113. The sign from Wigan Goods Yard has also survived and looks in particularly good order.
Mike Whalley.

WIGAN CENTRAL

Plate 114. Wigan Central Station seen long after closure c1971 along Station Road. After closure part of the station was used by Makinsons, Plumbers Merchants, as a showroom and offices. *Ian Isherwood.*

Wigan Central Station was a mixture of brick and timber construction, almost appearing haphazard in design. It was built in a sort of mock Tudor style with overhanging gables, flanked by a wooden pavilion which dominated the structure, particularly evident when viewed from lower level alongside the River Douglas. A domed balustraded cupola rose above the main gable apex, with a second cupola at lower level, both of which appeared completely out of character with Wigan's industrial economy. Tall chimney stacks with Tudor style patterned brickwork added to a confusion of purpose; was this really a railway station? In decay it looked even worse; a couple of sticks of dynamite would have improved it!

The proponents of the Wigan Junction Railways had intended this a through station, onward to the Fylde Coast via Longton and Preston they said. Unfortunately for them, their aspirations depended on the co-operation of the Lancashire & Yorkshire Railway whose approval was not forthcoming and without the necessary funds to do the job themselves it remained in isolation, often described as a 'backwater' of the Great Central, its single platform a testament to the failed, over-optimistic visions of its proposers, defeated by time and money.

All the grandiose plans of Watkin and his contemporaries had come to nought; Wigan was to remain an isolated outpost of the Great Central system. Nevertheless, an interesting outpost, despite its pretensions as a through route.

This was not quite the end of aspirations however, for, in 1907, a new plan was put forward by the Great Central as The Wigan & Heysham Railway, which would connect end on with the former Wigan Junction line at Central Station and pass through the same corridor as proposed in the 1883 Act. It would again cross the North Union, this time near Boar's Head and make connections with the Wigan Coal & Iron Company's Railway. Passing west of Preston by a viaduct over the River Ribble at Hesketh Bank, it would then join the Midland Railway's Leeds - Morecambe line at Lancaster. Blackpool was to be served by a branch line. Although giving a shorter route from Wigan to Blackpool than previous proposals it would have cost over £2,000,000 to construct. The time limit passed and this scheme also was allowed to lapse.

Plate 115. The exterior of Wigan Central Station as viewed from lower level on Orchard Street, alongside the River Douglas in May 1967.
John Sloane.

Plate 116. Taken from a similar viewpoint to John Sloane's photograph above, this is how the site of Wigan Central looks in 2013 having recently undergone a metamorphosis for the second time since its closure and is now the *Grand Arcade* shopping centre. The River Douglas still runs alongside Orchard Street but the embankment has been completely removed to accommodate earlier road works.
Author.

The extension of the Wigan Junction Railways from a point 198 yards south east of Darlington Street, crossed the latter and Warrington Lane, by an angled overbridge, then made its way through an area then known as 'Mill Meadow' before crossing the River Douglas immediately west of Mill Meadow and thence across Scholes by another overbridge to enter the station area proper. Here, before any construction of the station could begin the River Douglas, which meandered across open ground before passing under Crompton Street, had to be diverted and, firstly, a new bridge to take the diversion had to be constructed at the lower end of Crompton Street.

Work was not begun on the Wigan Station extension until early 1890, authorised by the Manchester, Sheffield & Lincolnshire Railways (Additional Powers) Act of 2nd August 1883. This Act envisaged extending the railway beyond Crompton Street to join the West Lancashire Railway at New Longton. En route, the railway would follow the Douglas Valley and going by way of Holme House, cross the North Union Railway just north of Ryland's Sidings where a short spur to the Wigan Coal & Iron Company's Railway at Standish would be made, a distance of approximately 3 3/4 miles. The only portion of this Act to be built was the short extension to Wigan Central Station and despite continued discussions about the line's viability, no work was ever carried out towards New Longton and the scheme was finally abandoned in 1896.

The first train arrived at Wigan Central, on the opening day, Monday 2nd October 1892, at 12.45pm. Aboard were the company directors and Lord Cross who, having cut the first sod at Ince, would now perform the opening ceremony.

In his speech, *the new station,* he says*, has a claim to beauty as well as convenience and adds greatly to the wealth of Wigan.* New roads had been constructed, from Millgate, Market Place and Crompton Street, giving adequate access to the station. The Mayor of Wigan comments; *out of what was once a wretched picture of barrenness and desolation, there has arisen a work of beauty and usefulness, and, the extension to the north will go forward with your Blackpool scheme.*

Fig 39. This extract from the second series Ordnance Survey was obviously made before any work on the Wigan Junction Railways extension to Central Station from Darlington Street had commenced, although ironically, it was published in 1892, the year that the new Central Station opened and was thus immediately out of date. Not until the revision in the early years of the twentieth century would the new station be part of official topography. The extension ran between the goods lines at Darlington Street, almost in a straight line before a slight curvature carried it over Scholes and thence onto the station site. Here, the River Douglas flowing southwards meanders its way through the middle of the site and under Crompton Street, necessitating diversion and a new bridge.

105

Plate 117. A deserted platform view at Wigan Central c.1935. To the left of the water tank part of Scholes Bridge can be seen; to the right of the tank is the ground frame seen in *Plates 121 & 122* and the small shunter/porters cabin. There's an ancient coach in the bay platform and adverts for Swan Vesta matches and Brylcream amongst others. *Author's Collection.*

Plate 118. Wigan Central Station nearing completion as the workmen pose for the photographer.

On October 8th 1892, the railway company applied for a refreshment licence to the Court and in reporting this application the *Wigan Observer* quotes room sizes as; First class refreshment room as 18ft x 16ft, and attached to that, and entered from the first class room was a large dining area 20ft 9in x 18ft 2in. A second class room, entered only from the platform at 18ft x 12ft, and at the back of this were offices and a kitchen. The licence was granted.

Leigh & Wigan Archives.

Fig 40. for comparison with *Fig 39* Page *105*, the updated Ordnance Survey shown here was revised in 1926. The River Douglas now passes under Crompton Street much lower down, near the junction with School Lane. The differing ground level upon which Central Station was built is seen to effect in **Plate 125,** the ground falling towards the river. Of particular interest to Wigan Rugby League supporters, Central Park is shown at the top, having only recently opened in 1902.

The land upon which Central Park had been built was, at the time, owned by the Manchester, Sheffield & Lincolnshire Railway having been purchased for the continuation of the route from Central Station to New Longton and, eventually, to Blackpool by way of the West Lancashire Railway's planned extension. These plans were abandoned in 1896.

According to an article in the *Wigan Observer,* the land was then known as 'Joe Hill's Field,' after a butcher of that name who used it for grazing cattle and, it was also used by travelling fairs and circuses. Councillor John Prescott, whose house overlooked the plot, put forward the idea that Wigan Rugby League Club should build their ground here and on 23rd January 1902, a meeting was held at the Public Hall in King Street. It was decided to negotiate for the lease of the land which had been offered by the railway company to the rugby club. The club committee raised £1,000 and began to prepare the field and on 6th September 1902, Central Park hosted its first ever game of Rugby League watched by a crowd of between 8,000 -10,000 spectators against Batley, winning by 14pts to 8pts.

The 'Old Shafts' shown north of Crompton Street are those of Alliance Colliery, leased by J. Marsden from 1888 and still working c1898, after Wigan Central opened. Had the extension to New Longton gone ahead, the railway would have to pass over these as it was planned to follow the Douglas Valley northwards towards Rylands Sidings, and why, having sold land for the construction of Central Park, did the Great Central Railway propose yet another extension, this time to Heysham through the same corridor in 1907?

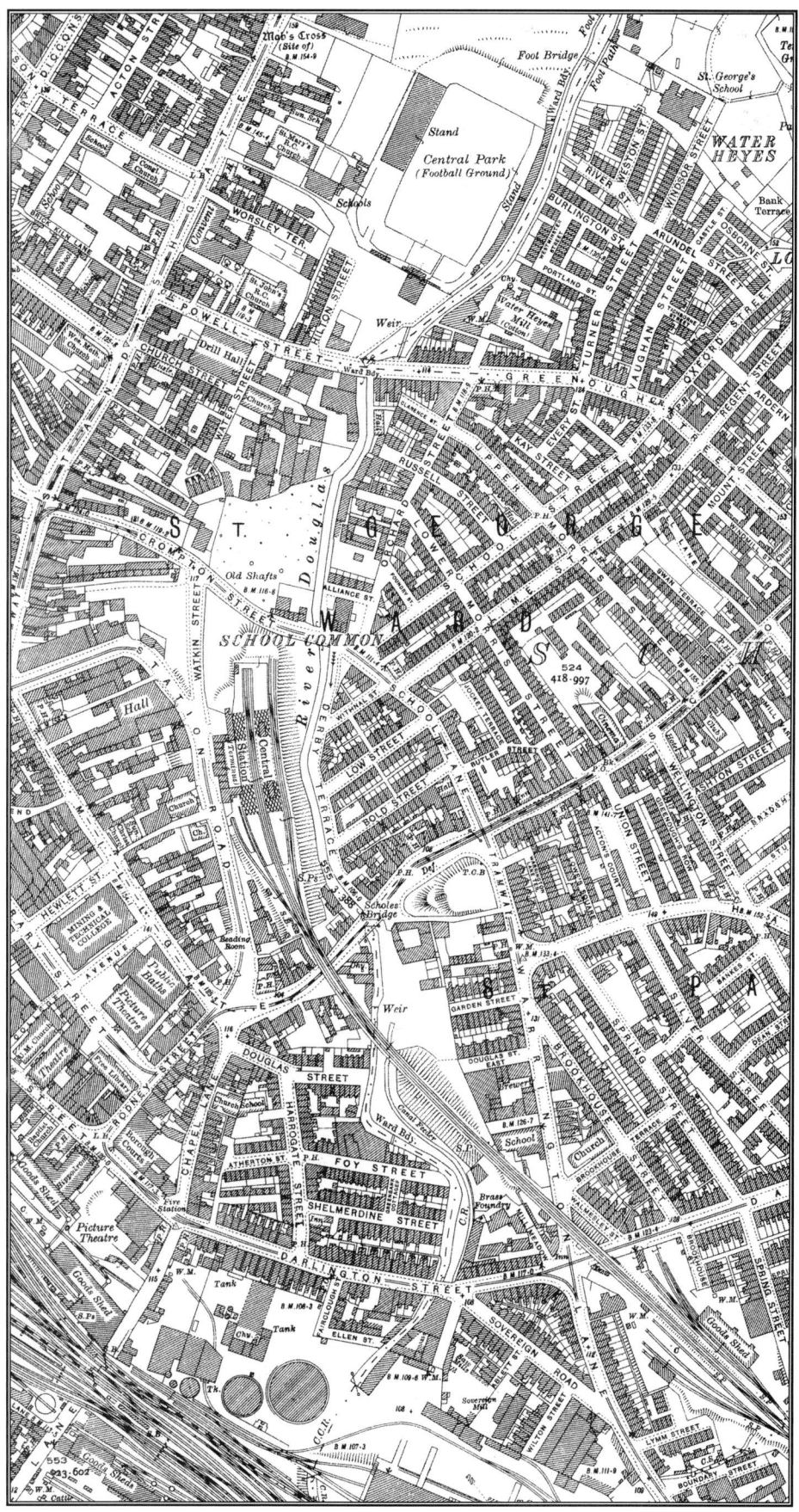

Plate 119. A 1950s view of Wigan Central. In 2009 the station area was being developed for the second time since closure, into retail shopping. The diverted River Douglas stands out well on the right of the station.

The site of Alliance Colliery was just across Crompton Street, directly opposite the station.

John Sloane Collection.

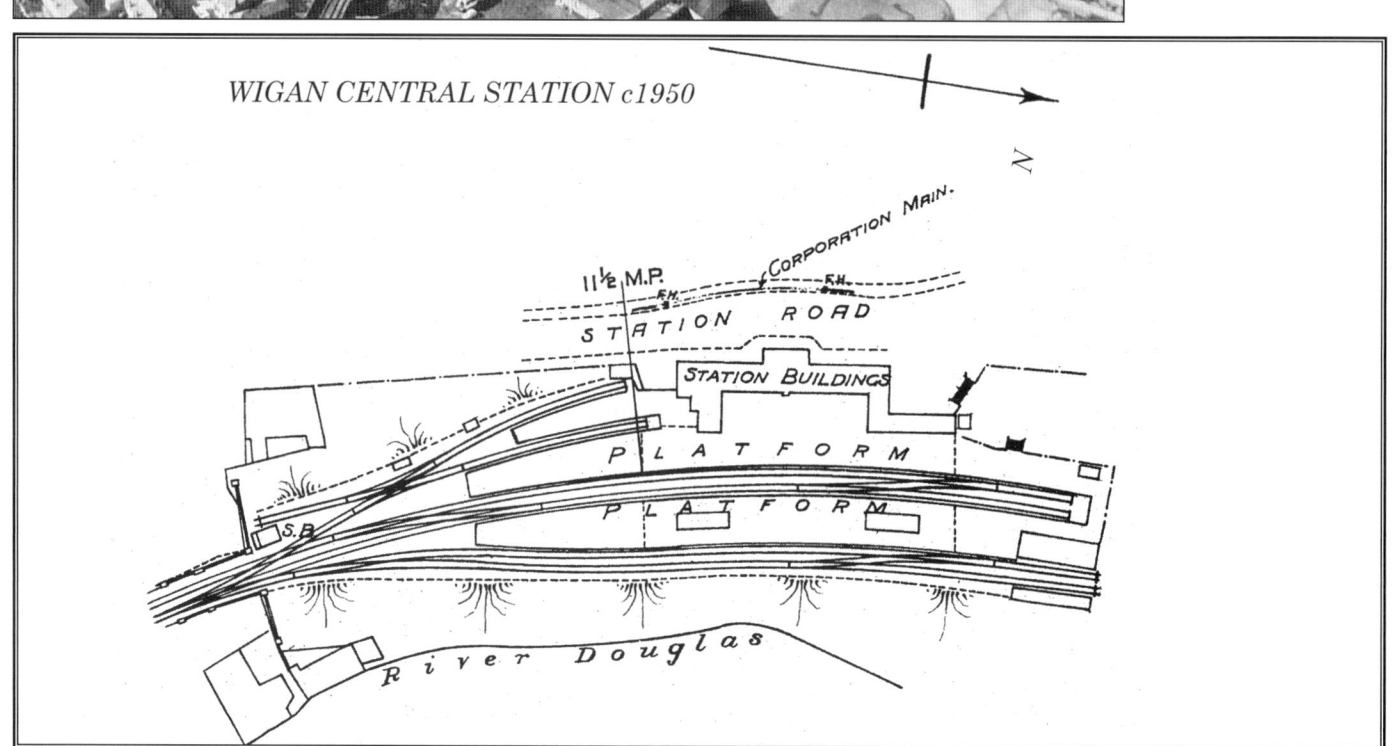

Fig 41. This map, showing Wigan Central signal box sited near Scholes Bridge, purports to be from the 1950s. However, this cannot be the case as the headshunt shown alongside the original signalbox, which was a Manchester, Sheffield & Lincolnshire Railway type having a 38 lever frame, was lifted some time after the 1907 Ordnance Survey update. The original signal box which opened on 28th September 1892 was closed in 1925/6 when single line operation was introduced. The much smaller cabin, seen in *Plate 122* opposite, must have been erected at a later date and is more of a shunter/porters cabin and sited much further away from the running lines than the original. This drawing is therefore, a copy, showing the original layout overprinted with the later date. See also **Fig 40.**

Plate 120. The crew of Ex - LMS Class '2' No.46434 have time for a chat before departure at Wigan Central on 29th December 1958. These lightweight 2-6-0 taper boilered engines were to an H.G.Ivatt design, entering service in 1946. *John Sloane Collection.*

Plates 121 & 122. The ground frame apparatus at Wigan Central about 1963. The Leading Porter, is using the locking bar release which allows him to use the point controlling levers so that an engine having arrived with its train can run-round its stock for the return journey.

Plate 123. Stanier 2-6-4T No.42465 has just arrived at Wigan Central from Manchester in June 1962. *Eddie Bellass.*

Plate 124. Stanier 2-6-4T No.42456 waits to depart with a Manchester Central service about 1960. In the years after nationalisation, the former ex LNER types were gradually replaced by ex-LMS or new BR Standard engines and the former could offer some smart acceleration on these lightly loaded trains. *John Sloane.*

Plate 125. A Stanier 2-6-4T is seen arriving at Wigan Central on 23rd June 1962.
Eddie Bellass.

Plate 126, below.
Wigan Central c1964/5. The first of the multi-storey housing blocks have already been built and more would follow in the Scholes area of Wigan. The station seems to be devoid of any rail traffic so this picture may well date from the period after passenger services had ceased in November 1964. *John Sloane Collection.*

111

Plate 127. An aerial view of Wigan c1971. Bottom left are the cooling towers of Westwood Power Station, its coal stocks and the generation house, alongside of which is the West Coast Main Line (W.C.M.L.). The former Lancashire & Yorkshire's (L&Y) line comes into the picture at lower right and meets the W.C.M.L. near the gasometers. The trackbed of the former Wigan Junction route also comes into the picture at bottom right and passes, firstly, under the Springs Branch, then an intermediate bridge before passing under Ince Green Lane. Next, the route can be seen to pass under the L&Y lines alongside of which is the site of Lower Ince Shed, where Kwik-Save Supermarket would later be built and, in the 1990s, housing. The remnants of Darlington Street Goods Yard can be clearly seen as can the station which appears to have found another use as a car park. Between Darlington Street and Scholes, to the right of the trackbed, more multi-storey blocks of flats have been built. Note also Central Park the former home of Wigan Rugby League Club, now hosting a supermarket.

The bare area between the Lancashire & Yorkshire line and the canal is that of the former Lower Coal Works, the industry of which had now passed into history. Today, the area is that of a regenerated forest, interspaced by a footpath or two, giving no inkling to the casual passer-by of its past.

John Sloane Collection.

Plate 128. A delapidated Wigan Central Station on 25th November 1964 as Stanier 2-6-4T No.42670 waits to depart for Manchester Central. The bay platform obviously hasn't been used for some time, in fact, some of the pointwork to it has been removed. I'm told fish vans were once unloaded here. *Peter Eckersley.*

Plate 129. The bridge over Scholes is seen on 29th July 1967 as Wigan Corporation service No.17 from Blackrod (Black Horse) via Meadowpit, Haigh, Aspull, Whelley and Scholes approaches. The bus will terminate on Station Road, outside Wigan Central Station.. The multistory flats were built by the contractors Rawlinson, the two blocks on the right already tenanted. *Allan Heyes.*

Plate 130. An unusual visitor to Wigan Central on 21st. September 1963 is Stanier '8F' No.48178. Although designed principally for heavy freight haulage, these engines were equally at home on passenger duties on which they were often rostered at weekends. On this occasion the '8F' is working a Locomotive Club of Great Britain (LCGB) special, 'The South Lancashire Limited Railtour.' The engines used on this tour were:- Class '4F' No.44501, '3F' No.47378 and '8F' Nos.48115 & 48178.

Beginning at Liverpool Road Goods Depot hauled by 48178, the train went via Eccles Junction - Tyldesley - Howe Bridge East to Atherton Bag Lane where 48115 was attached as banker to assist up the steep Chequerbent Bank to Hulton Sidings then onto Bolton Great Moor Street Station. There the '3F' was attached to work the train to Little Hulton. Unfortunately, the load was too much for the little engine which stalled on the climb from Great Moor Street and 48178 was summoned to bank the train and, after reaching Little Hulton, haul it back to Crook Street where it detached allowing 47378 to position the stock for departure, again hauled by 48178 working tender first.

Now, the route from Bolton was via Howe Bridge West Junction - Hindley Green - Bickershaw and Strangeways East Junctions and via Hindley South and Lower Ince to Wigan Central where the '8F' ran round. Working out of Wigan by the same route to Bickershaw, the Bickershaw Branch in its entirety was traversed to Pennington and Kenyon Junctions. The Bickershaw - Pennington section was, to quote from the LCGB publication, "the most decrepit track ever to be traversed by passenger rolling stock" with "water lapping the rails when crossing the (Leigh) Flash." Going now via Parkside East and Golborne Junctions, the special took the through lines via Bamfurlong Sidings to Amberswood, thereby taking the 'Whelley' route via Haigh Junction to Adlington. 48178's last duty was to drag the train via Horwich West Junction to Horwich Works.

At Horwich, No.44501 was attached and working via Horwich South - Hilton House - Crow Nest and Hindley No.2 Junctions, arrived at De Trafford Junction where, after running round, worked via Amberswood East Junction, taking the Wigan Junction route via Hindley South to Lowton St. Mary's. Another run-round at Lowton was necessary to traverse the branch to St. Helens Central and running round again as the turntable at St. Helens was not big enough to take a class '4', worked back to Lowton from where, via Glazebrook Moss and West Junctions, made its way to terminate at Manchester Central.

On the subject of specials, what is possibly the longest passenger train to traverse the route was an excursion to Scarborough in 1936, chartered by Brown & Haigh, wholesale clothiers of Wigan, for their staff. The train was composed of fourteen coaches:- Brake 1st; two third class open saloons; Great Central kitchen car; two third class open saloons; a six coach tourist set with buffet car and a 61ft van fitted out as a dance saloon. The Wigan platform could only accommodate six coaches, the passengers having to walk through the corridors to access their coach. The route taken was via Stockport, Penistone, Barnsley and a detour via Bolton-on-Dearne to York.

John Sloane Collection (The late Brian Fairhurst).

Plate 131. The clock on Wigan Central Station c1951 shows 12.50p.m. The train is the 1.10pm to Irlam and the boarding passengers, all men, are destined for the afternoon shift at the steel works. Special workers' trains ran from the early years over the Wigan Junction route to Low Hall and Wigan Junction Collieries.
Authors Collection, (Stations U.K.)

Plate 132. The Wigan Area Railfans Society (WARS) tour of 13th August 1966 arrived at Wigan Central at approximately 14.15hrs. However, by this date the track into the station was in the process of being lifted and the Wigan Goods signal box had closed on 10th May 1966. The photograph shows Stanier 'Mogul' No.42968 having been detached from its stock and in the process running round to depart at 14.30hrs on the last leg of the tour via Hindley South and Bickershaw Junctions where the engine will again run-round and proceed via Platt Bridge to Wigan North Western where the special will terminate. *Brian Taylor, courtesy of the Stanier Mogul Fund.*

British Railways Board

PUBLIC NOTICE

Withdrawal of Railway Passenger Services

The London Midland Area Board hereby gives notice, in accordance with Section 56 (7) of the Transport Act, 1962, that on and from Monday, 9th September, 1963, they propose to discontinue all railway passenger services between

WIGAN CENTRAL AND GLAZEBROOK

and from the following stations.

Lower Ince	Lowton St. Mary's
Hindley South	Culcheth
Bickershaw and Abram	Newchurch Halt
West Leigh and Bedford	

It appears to the Board that the following alternative services will be available :—

BY BUS

By road services operated by Wigan Corporation between

Wigan and Hindley   Service 3
Wigan and Abram   Service 12

By road services operated by Lancashire United Transport Ltd. between

Wigan and Bickershaw   Service 54

Negotiations for a through bus service to operate between Wigan and Irlam via Ince, Hindley, Abram, Lowton, Newchurch and Glazebrook are at present in progress.

OBJECTIONS

Any user of the rail service it is proposed to withdraw and any body representing such users, desirous of objecting to the proposed withdrawal of services, may lodge objections within six weeks of 20th July, i.e., not later than 2nd September, addressing any objections to the Secretary of the North Western Transport Users' Consultative Committee at Peter House, 2, Oxford Street, Manchester.

Note: If any objections are lodged within the period specified above, the closure cannot be proceeded with until the Transport Users' Consultative Committee has reported to the Minister and the Minister has given his consent (Section 56 (8) of the Transport Act 1962)

The first attempt at withdrawal of passenger services, as can be seen from the Public Notice above, was to be from Monday 9th September 1963. In the event, due to opposition in many quarters, a stay of execution was ordered by the Minister of Transport but this was only a prelude to a further closure attempt which was allowed. As a consequence, the total withdrawal of passenger services over the Manchester Central - Wigan Central took effect as from 2nd November 1964.

Former Railwayman Brian Kay remembers working over the route in the 1950s, maintaining it was a relatively easy line to work.

However, Brian's first encounter with the railway was not on the footplate but with the Carriage & Wagon Department. He, like most of us in those days, left school at 15 years of age and having made his way to the nearest Locomotive Depot, which in his case was 9E Trafford Park, went to see the Shed Foreman about a job, but at only 15, was told to come back when he had turned 16. The Foreman must have seen the disapointment in Brian's eyes and told him to go to the Cheshire Lines Goods Yard situated by the side of Manchester Central Station and ask to see the Carriage & Wagon Inspector. *If you get a job*, the Foreman said, *put in for a transfer as soon as you're 16.*

Brian was successful in his application at Manchester and was taken on as an oiler and greaser, and in the summer of 1949 was sent to Westleigh & Bedford on holiday relief work for two weeks.

The Carriage & Wagon Department at this particular location consisted of two old Great Central coach bodies just dumped near the lines, one of which can be seen in **Plate 49**, on the spur from Bickershaw Junction. The other was placed further round the curve, near the connection to Abram Nos 4&5 pits. One was used as a bothy, the other for storage.

Having duly arrived at Westleigh & Bedford by train he asked of the Station Master where the C&W depot was and duly reported to the wagon examiner (wheel tapper) who had a welcome cup of tea waiting. Whilst downing his tea, he was given a brief introduction of what his job was; oil all the full wagons, axle boxes etc; chalk the date on each wagon frame; and lastly, clean out the cabin. Wagons would come and go to many of the larger sidings like Glazebrook, Dewsnap, Partington or Warrington for marshalling or, in the case of loaded coal wagons, to the collieries' customers.

When Brian turned 16 in January 1950, he promptly put in his request to be transferred to the Motive Power Department and within a month found himself reporting to Trafford Park loco as an engine cleaner. Such was the shortage of manpower in those days, within months he was a passed fireman and had his first trip down the Wigan line.

He booked on duty at 3.10am to work the 4.40am freight from Trafford Park Sidings to Wigan, Darlington Street Goods and always, says Brian, *we had a 'J10' 0-6-0 on this job.* Brian always found the Wigan line easy to work, no heavy gradients, but plenty of speed restrictions and station stops when working Passenger turns.

It was always smokebox first when out, tender first coming back and the loco would be manned by three crews before returning to Trafford Park.

Recollecting, Brian recalls; *on the outward trip we would stop and pick up as required at Glazebrook and passing over Glazebrook Moss, through Culcheth to Lowton St. Mary's where we would pick up again. Having arrived at Wigan Goods about 7.30am, we would shunt in the yard until 8.04am and departing, make our way back to Glazebrook Sidings with just a brake van in tow where we would be relieved by a second crew at 8.37am. They would clean the fire and work one trip to Risley and then return to Glazebrook being relieved by a third set of men at 4.10pm. This turn would work engine and brake at 4.45pm to Irlam Margarine Factory, pick up three or four wagons and proceed first to Glazebrook at 5.35pm then to Lowton St. Mary's arriving about 6.28pm. It was virtually flat all the way and no hard work for the fireman.*

At Lowton, we worked onto the St. Helens line sidings to shunt and pick up any wagons from St. Helens but I never went any further down that line. We departed the sidings at 6.45 working tender first to Trafford Park arriving about 7.10pm where the shunter would uncouple and away to Trafford Park Loco. There we would clean the fire, coal and water the engine for its next turn.

It could be quite pleasant working to Wigan, passing over Glazebrook Moss, through Culcheth to Lowton St. Marys as it was virtually flat all the way and no hard work for the fireman. Sometimes we would pick up carriage stock from Lowton Yard if they were required for weekend specials. After Lowton it was up and down to Wigan, due mostly to mining subsidence, sometimes with small lakes in the dips but very interesting.

It was on the last turn in March 1955 and getting colder by the minute. Relieving the middle turn at Glazebrook Sidings we duly departed for Irlam to pick up two or three wagons and proceeded to Lowton for the wagons from St. Helens; sometimes these were from Pilkington's Glass Works. By this time the wind had picked up from the east and it started to snow.

We were travelling tender first with no sheet to cover the gap between tender and engine which turned the wind into gale force, something all engine crews will never forget and to say we were cold would be an understatement. I was huddled up against the firebox plate between firing and keeping a look-out for signals on my side of the footplate. Meanwhile, my driver was slowly turning blue with having to keep his head out looking for signals most of the time. Other trains had been delayed because of the weather and we arrived at Trafford Park Sidings over an hour late.

By the time we arrived on shed we were over our hours, no time to get coaled up, water the engine and clean the fire, so that was left to the shed men.

Plate 133. For some years after closure Wigan Central was used as a car park as seen here c1971, looking much delapidated.

Ian Isherwood.

Working the passenger trains could be a bit monotonous as the Trafford Park turns were all station stoppers out and back and usually we had an ex Great Central 'C12' or 'N5' when I first fired on the line. Later, in the 1950s, these were gradually replaced by ex-LMS types, Stanier 2-6-4 tank engines and the like. The Wigan crews had two Ivatt 2-6-0s Nos.46428 & 46434 but I never worked one of those engines.

It was on one of these passenger turns to Wigan Central where I had my most embarrassing moment, apart from stopping for blow-ups, not on the Wigan line though. Wigan Central had one platform with single line working and we would pick up the staff with a small annets key on the end of it from the signalman at Wigan Goods box, handing it back on the return.

On the particular day in question, we were entering the single line section into the station and it was the fireman's job to grab the staff from the signalman, and I dropped it! The driver applied the brakes but it was twenty or thirty yards before we stopped. Jumping off the engine I ran back to retrieve the staff but by this time the passengers had their heads out of the windows, all cheering, adding a few uncomplimentary remarks about my lack of ability to catch things.

There was not much else I recall happening to me on the Wigan line, nor did I hear of anything exciting happening to other crews. Although on one occasion we were working a Stanier 2-6-4 tank and this one was a poor steamer. Together with the number of station stops and speed restrictions we just managed to keep it going. My last turn before I left the railways was working another Stanier type over the Wigan line, but by then I'd had enough and did not feel bad about leaving the railway.

Ticket, courtesty, Tom Sherratt.

Fig 42. If the Wigan Junction Railways Act of 1875 had gone ahead the proposed station would have been north of Crompton Street, adjacent to Standishgate, Railway 'A' of the Act. It would have taken a slightly different route through Millgate and the vacant area alongside the River Douglas, the course of which should be noted prior to its deviation imposed by the later works for Wigan Central Station. Termination of Railway 'A' would have been at No.33 Standishgate, then in the ownership of a Mr. Edward Scott Esq; the tenant being a Mr. Charles Irvine. In the event, Railway 'A' was never to see the light of day and subsequently abandoned by the Manchester, Sheffield & Lincolnshire Railway's New Works, Act of 1881. In 1883, a further Act by the Company, the planned extension from Darlington Street to New Longton, and later, the Great Central Railway's proposal of 1907, would route the railway over the site of Alliance Colliery. For comparison, the proposed route of Railway 'A' has been drawn over the second series Ordnance Survey.

The original course of the River Douglas, seen here at bottom right would, in all probability, need no alteration to its course if this plan had gone ahead!

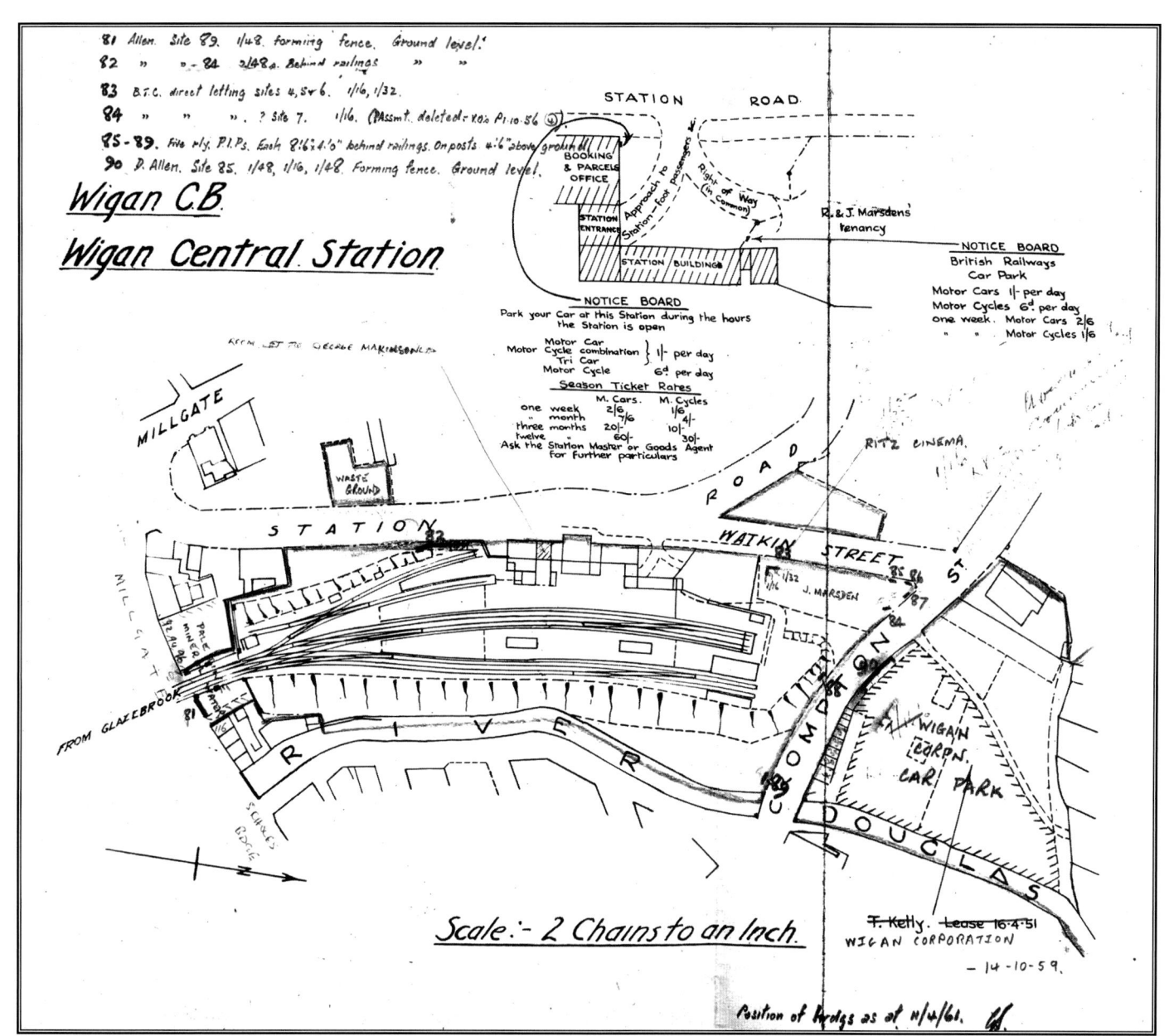

Fig 43. Wigan Central Station and the various car parks, rates thereof and other users, including Makinsons, who had let a portion of the station buildings. This is after the station had closed, the details overdrawn on an existing plan which would appear to be post W.W.II. Single line working was introduced c1925 after the grouping when the Great Central became part of the L.N.E.R. The token was obtained from Wigan Goods Yard box seen adjacent to the Leeds-Liverpool Canal in *Fig 36*. The notations as regards J.Marsden are interesting! Is this a descendant of Jamie Marsden who had owned Alliance Colliery on the opposite side of Crompton Street in the nineteenth century? The former shafts of the colliery were covered with circular flower beds for a number of years when in the ownership of Wigan Corporation as a car park.

Leigh & Wigan Archives.

Plate 134. Stanier 2-6-4T No. 42465 is about to shunt its stock into the sidings at Wigan Central on 23rd June 1962.

Note that the island platform originally intended for services beyond Wigan had the railway been extended to New Longton and the Fylde Coast, is still in situ. However, the island waiting rooms and their canopy, although remaining for many years, were demolished at an unknown date.

Eddie Bellass.

Plate 135. This is one of the very few photographs to show the island platform at Wigan Central in its original form and probably dates from the first decade of the twentieth century. There are adverts for Lyon's Tea and Sutton's Seeds among others. Most of the coaches seem to be of the third class, six wheeled variety. The coach, far right, appears to be a brake third, one of a number built by Ashburys between 1896/8 having guards duckets on either side. *John Ryan Collection.*

Plate 136. Another elevated view of Wigan Central from an unusual angle on an unknown date. The sparsity of road traffic is evident and demolition of the terraced housing opposite and adjacent to Wigan Little Theatre, seen at top centre, has yet to begin. My guess is that it's early 1950s. Behind the theatre is Alliance Street, so named because it was opposite the colliery of the same name the site of which seems to be in use as a coach park, much coveted earlier by the railway companies as a through route northwards.

John Sloane Collection.

Plate 137. The view north from the platform end as 42465 shunts its stock. Wigan Little Theatre can be seen on the extreme right.

Eddie Bellass.

Table 117. GLAZEBROOK, WIGAN AND ST. HELENS.

WEEKDAYS / SUNDAYS

[Timetable showing departure times from Liverpool (Central), Garston, Warrington (Central), Padgate, Glazebrook, Manchester (Central), Irlam and Cadishead, Glazebrook, Culcheth, Lowton St. Mary's, West Leigh and Bedford, Bickershaw and Abram, Hindley and Platt Bridge, Lower Ince, Wigan (Central), Lowton St. Mary's, Golborne, Ashton-in-Makerfield, Haydock, St. Helens (Central) — reverse direction below]

Notes:

- **A** Change at Irlam.
- **B** Fridays and Saturdays only.
- **C** On Saturdays leaves Garston 1.13 p.m.
- **E** On Saturdays leaves Glazebrook 11.16, arrives Padgate 11.24 and Warrington 11.29 a.m.
- **F** One class only except on Saturdays.
- **FO** Fridays only.
- **FSX** Fridays and Saturdays excepted.
- **H** Change at Halewood.
- **M** Change at Warrington.
- **J** Change at Hunt's Cross, Warrington and Glazebrook.
- **SO** Saturdays only.
- **SX** Saturdays excepted.
- **T** Change at Glazebrook.
- **X** One class only.

Passengers between Liverpool, Warrington, Wigan and St. Helens change at Glazebrook in each direction.

L.N.E.R Timetable 11th September 1933 to 30th April 1934

CHEAP DAY RETURN FARES

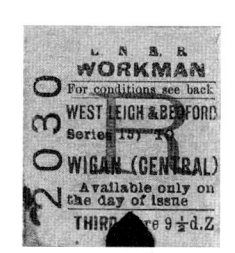

	Ashton-in-Makerfield		Bickershaw & Abram		Culcheth		Flixton		Glazebrook		Golborne		Haydock		Hindley & Platt Bridge		Irlam	
FROM	1st	3rd	1st	3rd	1st	3rd	1st	3rd	1st	3rd	1st	3rd	1st	3rd	1st	3rd	1st	3rd
1 Ashton-in-Makerfield	—	—	—	—	—	—	2/9	1/8	2/-	1/5	—/5	—/3	—/5	—/3	—	—	2/3	1/4
2 Bickershaw & Abram	—	—	—	—	1/2	—/9	2/6	1/6	1/11	1/1	—/9	—/6	—/10	—/6	—/3	—/2	2/1	1/3
3 Culcheth	1/3	—/9	1/2	—/9	—	—	1/6	—/11	—/9	—/6	1/1	—/8	1/6	—/11	1/1	—/9	1/1	—/8
4 Flixton	2/9	1/8	2/6	1/6	1/6	—/11	—	—	—/11	—/6	2/4	1/5	3/1	1/10	2/6	1/6	—/8	—/4
5 Glazebrook	2/-	1/5	1/11	1/1	—/9	—/6	—/11	—/6	—	—	1/7	1/-	2/4	1/5	2/-	1/3	—/6	—/5
6 Golborne	—/5	—/3	—/9	—/6	1/-	—/10	2/4	1/5	1/7	1/-	—	—	1/-	—/6	—/10	—/6	1/10	1/1
7 Haydock	—/5	—/3	—/10	—/6	1/5	—/11	3/1	1/10	2/4	1/5	1/-	—/6	—	—	1/3	—/9	2/8	1/7
8 Hindley & Platt Bridge	—	—	—/3	—/2	1/1	—/9	2/6	1/6	2/-	1/3	—/10	—/6	1/3	—/9	—	—	2/4	1/5
9 Irlam	2/3	1/4	2/1	1/3	1/1	—/8	—/8	—/4	—/6	—/5	1/10	1/1	2/8	1/7	2/4	1/5	—	—/8
10 Lower Ince	—	—	—/7	—/4	1/7	—/11	2/9	1/8	2/3	1/4	—/11	—/7	1/5	—/10	—/4	—/2	2/8	1/7
11 Lowton St. Mary's	—/10	—/6	—/6	—/4	—/6	—/4	1/11	1/2	1/3	—/9	—/5	—/3	—/10	—/6	1/-	—/8	1/6	—/11
12 Manchester (Central)	4/-	2/5	3/1	1/10	2/5	1/6	—	—	—	—	3/4	2/-	4/4	2/7	3/3	2/-	—	—
13 St. Helens	1/1	—/8	—	—	2/1	1/3	3/8	2/11	3/-	1/10	1/6	—/11	—/6	—/4	2/3	1/4	3/3	2/-
14 Trafford Park & Stretford	3/4	2/-	3/-	1/10	2/1	1/3	—	—	—	—	2/11	1/9	3/10	2/3	2/10	1/9	—	—
15 Urmston	2/11	1/9	2/10	1/9	1/9	1/-	—	—	—/8	—/4	2/8	1/7	3/4	2/-	2/11	1/10	—/5	—/3
16 West Leigh & Bedford	—/9	—/6	—/4	—/3	—/9	—/6	2/3	1/4	1/8	1/-	—/6	—/4	1/-	—/8	—/6	—/4	1/10	1/1
17 Wigan (Central)	—/8	—/8	—/5	—/3	1/10	1/1	3/3	2/-	2/6	1/6	1/1	—/8	—/7	—/4	2/9	1/8	—	—

	Lower Ince		Lowton St. Mary's		Manchester (Central)		St. Helens		Trafford Park & Stretford		Urmston		West Leigh & Bedford		Wigan (Central)	
FROM	1st	3rd	1st	3rd	1st	3rd	1st	3rd	1st	3rd	1st	3rd	1st	3rd	1st	3rd
1 Ashton-in-Makerfield	—	—	—/10	—/6	4/-	2/5	1/1	—/8	3/4	2/-	2/11	1/9	—/9	—/6	—/8	—/8
2 Bickershaw & Abram	—/7	—/4	—/6	—/4	3/1	1/10	—	—	3/-	1/10	2/10	1/9	—/4	—/3	—/5	—/3
3 Culcheth	1/7	—/11	—/6	—/4	2/5	1/6	2/1	1/3	2/1	1/3	1/9	1/-	—/9	—/6	1/10	1/1
4 Flixton	3/1	1/10	1/11	1/1	—	—	3/8	2/3	—	—	—	—	2/3	1/4	3/3	2/-
5 Glazebrook	2/4	1/5	1/3	—/9	—	—	3/-	1/10	—	—	—/7	—/4	1/8	1/-	2/6	1/6
6 Golborne	—	—	—/5	—/3	3/4	2/-	1/6	—/11	2/11	1/9	2/8	1/7	—/6	—/4	1/1	—/8
7 Haydock	—	—	1/3	—/9	4/4	2/7	—/6	—/4	3/10	2/3	3/4	2/-	1/-	—/8	—/7	—/4
8 Hindley & Platt Bridge	—/4	—/3	—/10	—/6	3/3	2/-	2/3	1/4	3/3	2/-	2/11	1/10	—/6	—/4	—/7	—/4
9 Irlam	2/8	1/7	1/6	—/11	—	—	3/3	2/-	—	—	—/5	—/3	1/10	1/1	2/9	1/8
10 Lower Ince	—	—	1/2	—/9	3/7	2/2	1/9	1/-	3/6	2/-	2/10	1/9	—/4	—/3	—/3	—/2
11 Lowton St. Mary's	1/2	—/9	—	—	2/5	1/6	1/10	1/1	2/1	1/3	2/-	1/-	—/6	—/4	1/5	—/10
12 Manchester (Central)	3/7	2/2	2/5	1/6	—	—	4/7	2/9	—	—	—	—	2/6	1/6	3/9	2/3
13 St. Helens	—	—	1/10	1/1	4/7	2/9	—	—	4/4	2/7	4/-	2/4	2/-	1/3	1/1	—/8
14 Trafford Park & Stretford	3/8	2/2	2/5	1/6	—	—	4/4	2/7	—	—	—	—	2/6	1/6	3/9	2/3
15 Urmston	3/3	1/9	2/-	1/3	—	—	4/-	2/4	—	—	—	—	2/-	1/3	3/4	2/-
16 West Leigh & Bedford	—/10	—/6	—/5	—/3	2/6	1/6	2/-	1/3	2/6	1/6	2/-	1/3	—	—	1/1	—/8
17 Wigan (Central)	—/3	—/2	1/5	—/10	3/9	2/3	1/1	—/8	3/9	2/3	3/4	2/-	1/1	—/8	—	—

Tickets, Courtesy, Tom Sherratt.

L.N.E.R. MONTHLY RETURN — WIGAN CEN or Intermediately — BICKERSHAW & ABR'M — Available one month from date of issue. 3rd. 10½d.Z — For conditions see back. — 4844

L.N.E.R. MONTHLY RETURN — BICKERSHAW & ABR'M — TO — WIGAN (CENTRAL) or Intermediately — Available one month from date of issue. 3rd. 10½d.Z — For conditions see back. — 4844

L.N.E.R. WORKMAN — WEST LEIGH & BEDFORD — Series 151 — TO — WIGAN (CENTRAL) — Available only on the day of issue. THIRD fare 9½d.Z — 2030

Table 149a — GLAZEBROOK, WIGAN, and St. HELENS

The timetable for May-September 1948. The dismal passenger service to/from St. Helens is evidence of a railway on decline.

Plate 138. Stanier 2-6-4T No.42465, having detached from its train is about to run round and shunt its stock into the sidings in June 1962. The guard seems to pay little attention to all this, perhaps more interested in brewing up!

Eddie Bellass.

Train Movements mid 1950s

Down line Weekdays

AM/PM	FROM	DEPT		ARR	DEPT/PASS	TO	ARR		TYPE
AM	Springs Branch Loco	4.15	Hindley South		4.28	Wigan Cen.	4.35		G (LE)
AM	Guide Bridge	3.50	Lowton St. Mary's	5.15		Lowton St. Mary's			H
AM	Springs Branch Loco	5.20	Hindley South		5.33	Wigan Cen.	5.43		G (LE)
AM	Springs Branch Loco	5.25	Hindley South		5.40	Wigan Goods	5.46		G (LE)
AM	Springs Branch Loco	6.00	Hindley South		6.12	Wigan Goods	6.16		G (LE)
AM	Wigan Goods	6.13				Wigan Cen.	6.15		C (ECS)
AM	Wigan Goods	6.24				Wigan Cen.	6.25		C (ECS)
AM	Wigan Goods	6.59				Wigan Cen.	7.01	SX	C (ECS)
AM	Irlam	6.13	Lowton St. Mary's	6.30	6.31	Wigan Cen.	6.49		B
AM	Glazebrook Sidings	6.25	Lowton St. Mary's	6.45	7.10	Wigan Goods	7.30	MO	H
AM	Trafford Park Sidings	4.40	Lowton St. Mary's	6.45	7.10	Wigan Goods	7.30	MSX	H
AM	Trafford Park Sidings	4.40	Lowton St. Mary's	6.45	7.10	Wigan Goods	7.55	SO	H
AM			Lowton St. Mary's		7.30	St. Helens	8.00		K
AM	Glazebrook	7.24	Lowton St. Mary's	7.38	7.39	Wigan Cen.	7.54		B
AM	Manchester Central	7.38	Lowton St. Mary's	8.19	8.21	Wigan Cen.	8.39		B
AM	Manchester Central	8.00	Lowton St. Mary's	8.42		Lowton St. Mary's			B
AM			Lowton St. Mary's		8.50	West Leigh & Bedford	8.55	SO	G (LE)
AM	Irlam	9.02	Lowton St. Mary's	9.14		Lowton St. Mary's			C (ECS)
AM			Lowton St. Mary's		9.17	Wigan Cen.	9.35		B
AM			West Leigh & Bedford		9.26	Wigan Banfurlong Sidings	10.00	SO	K
AM	Glazebrook Sidings	9.23	Lowton St. Mary's		9.46	West Leigh & Bedford	9.52	SO	J
AM	Widnes Central	8.54	Lowton St. Mary's		9.48	Long Meg Lozonby M.R.	10.15pm	SX	F
AM			Lowton St. Mary's		9.50	West Leigh & Bedford	9.12	SX	K
AM	Desford (Nr. Leicester)	5.45	Lowton St. Mary's		9.56	Blackpool North	11.13	SO	A
AM	Widnes Central	8.54	Lowton St. Mary's		9.48	Long Meg Lozonby M.R.	10.15pm	SO	F
AM			Lowton St. Mary's		10.00	St. Helens	10.30	SO	K
AM	Irlam	10.01	Lowton St. Mary's	10.18	10.19	Wigan Cen.	10.37		B
AM	Glazebrook Sidings	10.10	Lowton St. Mary's		10.29	West Leigh & Bedford	10.35	SX	J
AM			West Leigh & Bedford		10.30	Wigan Banfurlong Sidings	10.58	SX	K
AM	Sheffield Midland	8.50	Lowton St. Mary's		10.35	Blackpol Central	12.13	SO	A
AM	Nottingham Midland	7.25	Lowton St. Mary's		10.53	Blackpool North	12.09	SO	A
AM			West Leigh & Bedford		11.05	Springs Branch Loco	11.12	SX	G (LE)
AM			Lowton St. Mary's		11.30	St. Helens	12:00	SX	H
AM	Partington	10.25	West Leigh & Bedford	11.33	11.43	Edge Green Colliery (Golborne)	11.53		K
AM			West Leigh & Bedford		11.45	Wigan Goods	12.00	SO	G(EBV)
PM			Lowton St. Mary's		12.25	Wigan Cen.	12.43	SO	B
PM	Trafford Park	11.50	Lowton St. Mary's	12.21				SO	B
PM	Irlam	12.20	Lowton St. Mary's	12.38	12.40	Wigan Cen.	12.58	SO	B
PM			Lowton St. Mary's		12.52	Springs Branch Loco	1.10	SO	G (LE)
PM	Wigan Goods	12.33				Wigan Cen.	12.35	SX	G(LE)
PM	Partington Ju.	12.05	West Leigh & Bedford	12.52				SX	G(EBV)
PM	Atherton Bag Lane	12.40	Hindley South	1.03	1.05	Kerarsley		SX	J
PM			Lowton St. Mary's		1.08	Springs Branch Loco	1.25	SX	G (LE)
PM	Manchester Central	12.33	Lowton St. Mary's	1.12	1.14	Wigan Cen.	1.32		B
PM	Leicester LR	10.05	Lowton St. Mary's		1.38	Blackpool North		SO	A
PM	Wigan Goods	1.43				Wigan Cen.	1.45	SO	G(LE)
PM	Irlam	1.33	Lowton St. Mary's	1.46				SO	C (ECS)
PM	Atherton Bag Lane	1.30	Hindley South	1.53	1.55	Kerarsley		SO	J
PM	Irlam	2.15	Lowton St. Mary's	2.32	2.33	Wigan Cen.	2.51		B
PM	Warrington	2.35	Glazebrook Moss Ju.	2.53	2.55	Glazebrook Sidings	3.01	SO	G(EBV)
PM	Lowton St. Mary's	3.00(LE)	West Leigh & Bedford	3.05	3.15(EB)V	Wigan Goods	3.32	SX	G
PM	Wigan Goods	3.20				Wigan Cen.	3.22	SO	G(Pcls)
PM	Springs Branch Loco	3.05	Hindley South		3.18	Wigan Goods	3.23	SX	G (LE)
PM			Lowton St. Mary's		3.26	Wigan Cen.	3.45	SX	B
PM			Lowton St. Mary's		3.30	Springs Branch Loco	3.47	SO	G (LE)
PM	Partington Ju.	3.32	Hindley South	4.16	4.17	Springs Branch Loco	4.24	SX	G (LE)
PM	Manchester Central	3.33	Lowton St. Mary's	4.17	4.18	Wigan Cen.	4.36		B
PM	Springs Branch Loco	4.25	Hindley South		4.39	Wigan Cen.	4.45	SO	G (LE)
PM	Warrington	4.31	Glazebrook Moss Ju.	4.46	4.48	Glazebrook Sidings	4.54	FSX	G(EBV)
PM			Lowton St. Mary's		5.25	West Leigh & Bedford	5.30	SX	G (LE)
PM	Partington	5.09	Lowton St. Mary's	5.30	5.31	Wigan Cen.	5.49	SX	B
PM	Irlam	5.15	Lowton St. Mary's	5.32	5.33	Wigan Cen.	5.51	SO	B
PM	Irlam	5.25	Lowton St. Mary's	5.42	5.44	Wigan Cen.	6.02	SX	B
PM	Trafford Park	5.12	Lowton St. Mary's	5.49		Lowton St. Mary's		SX	B
PM	Risley	5.45	Lowton St. Mary's	6.00	6.02	Wigan Cen.	6.20	SX	B
PM			West Leigh & Bedford	6.20		Springs Branch Loco	6.35	SX	G (LE)
PM	Glazebrook Sidings	6.06	Lowton St. Mary's	6.28				SX	G(EBV)
PM	Manchester Central	6.05	Lowton St. Mary's	6.46	6.49	Wigan Cen.	7.07		B
PM	Manchester Central	7.10	Lowton St. Mary's	7.50	7.51	Wigan Cen.	8.09		B
PM	Guide Bridge	7.05	Lowton St. Mary's	8.27				SO	H

Down line Weekdays Con't.

AM/PM	FROM	DEPT		ARR	DEPT/PASS	TO	ARR		TYPE
PM	Manchester Central	7.10	Lowton St. Mary's	7.50	7.51	Wigan Cen.	8.09		B
PM	Guide Bridge	7.05	Lowton St. Mary's	8.27				SO	H
PM	Warrington	8.02	Lowton St. Mary's		8.40	West Leigh & Bedford	8.46	SX	J
PM			Lowton St. Mary's		8.45	Springs Branch Loco	9.03	SO	G (LE)
PM	Springs Branch Loco	8.33	Hindley South		8.46	Wigan Goods	8.51	SO	G (LE)
PM	Manchester Central	8.30	Lowton St. Mary's	9.10	9.11	Wigan Cen.	9.29		B
PM	Glazebrook Sidings	8.30	Lowton St. Mary's		9.16	West Leigh & Bedford	9.21	SX	J
PM			West Leigh & Bedford		9.35	Springs Branch Loco	9.50	SX	G (LE)
PM	Irlam	10.16	Lowton St. Mary's	10.33	10.34	Wigan Cen.	10.52		B
PM	Guide Bridge	9.35	Lowton St. Mary's	10.50				SX	H
PM	Glazebrook Sidings	11.10	Lowton St. Mary's	11.28	11.35	Springs Branch Loco	11.53	SX	G (LE)
PM	Irlam	11.54	Lowton St. Mary's	12.09	12.10	Wigan Cen.	12.21	SO	B

Down Line Sundays

AM/PM	FROM	DEPT		ARR	DEPT/PASS	TO	ARR		TYPE
AM	Springs Branch Loco	4.25				Wigan Cen.	4.45		G (LE)
AM	Springs Branch Loco	5.25				Wigan Cen.	5.50		G (LE)
AM	Irlam	6.13	Lowton St. Mary's	6.27	6.28	Wigan Cen.	6.42		B
AM	Irlam	7.55	Lowton St. Mary's	8.09	8.10	Wigan Cen.	8.24		B
PM	Wigan Goods	12.08				Wigan Cen.	12.10		G (LE)
PM	Irlam	2.15	Lowton St. Mary's	2.32	2.33	Wigan Cen.	2.47		B
PM	Manchester Central	5.05	Lowton St. Mary's	5.44	5.45	Wigan Cen.	5.59		B
PM	Manchester Central	8.42	Lowton St. Mary's	9.21	9.22	Wigan Cen.	9.36		B
PM	Manchester Central	9.57	Lowton St. Mary's	10.37	10.38	Wigan Cen.	10.52		B

Up line Weekdays.

AM/PM	FROM	DEPT		ARR	DEPT/PASS	TO	ARR		TYPE
AM	Wigan Cen.	5.04	Lowton St. Mary's	5.24	5.25	Irlam	5.43		B
AM	Wigan Cen.	6.10	Lowton St. Mary's	6.28	6.29	Manchester Central	7.15		B
AM	Wigan Cen.	6.21	Lowton St. Mary's	6.39	6.40	Partington	7.01		B
AM	Wigan Cen.	6.34	Lowton St. Mary's		6.49	Manchester Central	7.24		B
AM	Springs Branch Loco	6.30	Lowton St. Mary's	7.00					G (LE)
AM	Wigan Cen.	6.57	Lowton St. Mary's	7.15	7.16	Risley	7.33	SX	B
AM	Wigan Cen.	7.06	Lowton St. Mary's	7.24	7.25	Irlam	7.43		B
AM	Springs Branch Loco	7.40	Lowton St. Mary's		8.05	Glazebrook Sidings	8.25	SO	G (LE)
AM	Wigan Goods	8.04	Lowton St. Mary's		8.21	Glazebrook Sidings	8.37	SX	G(EBV)
AM	Wigan Cen.	8.04	Lowton St. Mary's	8.22	8.23	Irlam	8.40		B
AM	Springs Branch Loco	8.00	Lowton St. Mary's	8.30					G (LE)
AM	Wigan Goods	8.18	Lowton St. Mary's	8.35	8.52	Glazebrook Sidings	9.08	SO	G(EBV)
AM	St. Helens	9.00	Lowton St. Mary's	9.25					K
AM	Wigan Cen.	9.00	Lowton St. Mary's	9.17	9.18	Manchester Central	9.59		B
AM	Springs Branch Loco	9.45	Lowton St. Mary's	10.11				SX	G (LE)
AM	Springs Branch Loco	10.00	West Leigh & Bedford	10.21				SX	G (LE)
AM	Bamfurlong Sidings	10.01	Hindley South	10.20				SO	G (LE)
AM	Blackpool N	9.35	Lowton St. Mary's		10.51	Nottingham Midland	2.17	SO	A
AM	Adlington Ju. Lancs	9.30	Lowton St. Mary's		10.43	Widnes Central	11.40	MX	F
AM	Blackpool N	10.25	Lowton St. Mary's		11.39	Leicester L Rd.	2.45	SO	A
AM	Hindley South	11.00	West Leigh & Bedford	11.15				SO	K
AM	West Leigh & Bedford	11.00				Partington Ju.	11.36	SX	H
AM	Wigan Goods	11.00				Springs Branch Loco	11.13		G (LE)
AM	Wigan Cen.	11.30	Lowton St. Mary's	11.48	11.49	Irlam	12.06	SO	B
AM	West Leigh & Bedford	11.50	Lowton St. Mary's	11.55				SO	G (LE)
AM	Wigan Banfurlong Sidings	11.30	West Leigh & Bedford	12.35				SX	K
PM	Springs Branch Loco	12.05	West Leigh & Bedford	12.10				SO	G (LE)
PM	St.Helens	12.05	Lowton St. Mary's	12.55				SX	K
PM	Aston in M	12.40	Lowton St. Mary's	11.50				SO	K
PM	Wigan Cen.	12.55	Lowton St. Mary's	1.13	1.19	Irlam	1.37	SO	B
PM			Lowton St. Mary's		12.40	Manchester Central	1.22	SO	B
PM	St.Helens	1.00	Lowton St. Mary's	1.25				SO	K
PM	St.Helens	1.00	Lowton St. Mary's	1.25				SO	K
PM	Wigan Cen.	1.00	Lowton St. Mary's	1.18	1.19	Irlam	1.37	SX	B
PM	Wigan Cen.	1.08	Wigan Goods	1.10				SO	C{ECS)
PM	Wigan Cen.	1.40	Wigan Goods	1.42				SO	G (LE)
PM	Ashton in Makerfield	1.50	Lowton St. Mary's	2.30				SX	K
PM	Wigan Cen.	2.00	Lowton St. Mary's	2.18	2.20	Manchester Central	3.00		B
PM	Wigan Goods	2.10	Lowton St. Mary's	2.35	3.25	Dewsnap(Guide Bridge)	4.55	SO	E
PM	Springs Branch Loco	2.35	Lowton St. Mary's	3.01					G (LE)
PM	Wigan Cen.	3.05	Wigan Goods	3.07				SO	G (LE)

Up line Weekdays Con't.

AM/PM	FROM	DEPT		ARR	DEPT/PASS	TO	ARR		TYPE
PM	Wigan Cen.	3.40	Lowton St. Mary's	3.58	4.00	Irlam	4.22	SX	B
PM	Blackpol Central	1.50	Lowton St. Mary's		3.21	Sheffield Midland	5.06	SO	A
PM	Blackpool North	2.45	Lowton St. Mary's		4.02	Leicester L Rd.	7..35	SO	A
PM	Wigan Cen.	4.00	Lowton St. Mary's	4.14	4.15	Partington	4.38	SX	B
PM	St.Helens	4.00	Lowton St. Mary's	4.25				SX	K
PM	Wigan Cen.	4.15	Lowton St. Mary's	4.33	4.35	Irlam	4.52	SO	B
PM	Springs Branch Loco	4.25	Lowton St. Mary's		4.47	Risley	5.07	SX	G (LE)
PM	Wigan Goods	4.55				Wigan N.W.	5.25	SO	C{PCLS)
PM	Wigan Cen.	5.05	Lowton St. Mary's	5.23	5.44	Manchester Central	6.04		B
PM	Wigan Goods	5.15	Lowton St. Mary's	5.55	6.15	Dewsnap(Guide Bridge)	8.05	SX	E
PM			Lowton St. Mary's		6.10	Irlam	6.28	SX	B
PM	West Leigh & Bedford	5.55	Wigan Goods	5.57				SX	C{ECS)
PM	Wigan Cen.	6.00	Lowton St. Mary's	6.10	6:30	Warrington	7.13	SX	H
PM	Wigan Goods	6.03	Wigan Goods	6.05				SO	C{ECS)
PM	Wigan Goods	6.10				Springs Branch Loco	6.23	SO	G (LE)
PM	Wigan Goods	6.10	Lowton St. Mary's	6.45	7.10	Glazebrook Sidings	7.45	SX	H
PM	Wigan Cen.	;6.10	Wigan Goods	6.12				SX	C{ECS)
PM	Wigan Goods	6.17				Springs Branch Loco	6.30	SX	G (LE)
PM	Wigan Cen.	6.40	Wigan Goods	6.42				SX	C{ECS)
PM	Wigan Cen.	7.38	Lowton St. Mary's	8.01	8.02	Manchester Central	8.41	SX	B
PM	Wigan Cen.	7.38	Lowton St. Mary's	7.59	8.02	Manchester Central	8.41	SO	B
PM	Wigan Goods	8.05	Lowton St. Mary's	8.20				SX	C{ECS)
PM	Wigan Cen.	9.05	Lowton St. Mary's	9.23	9.24	Manchester Central	10.07		B
PM	Wigan Goods	9.25				Irlam	9.55	SO	C{ECS)
PM			Lowton St. Mary's		9.38	Irlam	9.55	SX	C{ECS)
PM	Wigan Cen.	9.45				Springs Branch Loco	10.00	SO	G (LE)
PM	Wigan Cen.	9.45	Wigan Goods	9.47				SX	C{ECS)
PM	West Leigh & Bedford	9.45	Lowton St. Mary's		9.55	Glazebrook Sidings	10.20	SX	H
PM	Wigan Goods	10.05				Wigan N.W.	10.37	SX	C{PCLS)
PM	Wigan Cen.	10.55				Springs Branch Loco	11.29	SX	G (LE)
PM	Wigan Cen.	11.12	Lowton St. Mary's	11.30	11.31	Irlam	11.46	SO	B

Up Line Sundays

AM/PM	FROM	DEPT		ARR	DEPT/PASS	TO	ARR	TYPE
AM	Wigan Cen.	12.35				Springs Branch Loco	12.50	G (LE)
AM	Wigan Cen.	5.15	Lowton St. Mary's	5.29	5.30	Irlam	5.44	B
AM	Wigan Cen.	6.26	Lowton St. Mary's	6.40	6.41	Manchester Central	7.18	B
AM	Wigan Cen.	7.00	Lowton St. Mary's	7.14	7.16	Irlam	7.31	B
AM	Wigan Cen.	8.35	Wigan Goods	8.37				G (LE)
PM	Wigan Cen.	12.53	Lowton St. Mary's	1.07	1.08	Irlam	1.25	B
PM	Wigan Cen.	4.41	Lowton St. Mary's	4.55	4.56	Manchester Central	5.37	B
PM	Wigan Cen.	9.00	Lowton St. Mary's	9.14	9.15	Manchester Central	9.56	B
PM	Wigan Cen.	9.50				Springs Branch Loco	10.05	G (LE)
PM	Wigan Cen.	11.00	Wigan Goods	11.02				C{ECS)
PM			Wigan Goods		11.10	Springs Branch Loco	11.23	G (LE)

Compiled by Brian Kay

Plate 139. Class 'J10' No.65170 takes water at Wigan Central on 23rd August 1952. These engines were introduced in 1896 to a design by Pollitt for the Manchester, Sheffield & Lincolnshire Railway. Renumbered as 850 by the Great Central Railway, it was again renumbered, firstly to 9850, and later, as 5170 by the London & North Eastern Railway, finally becoming 65170 at Nationalization in 1948.
John Sloane Collection (H.C.Casserley).

BIBLIOGRAPHY

A Lancashire Triangle Part One. D.J.Sweeney. Triangle Publishing 1996.
The Wigan Branch Railway, D.J.Sweeney. Triangle Publishing 2008.
The Lancashire Union Railway, D.J.Sweeney. Triangle Publishing 2010.
Great Central, George Dow, Locomotive Publishing Ltd., 1962.
The Industrial Railways of the Wigan Coalfield Part One. C.H.A.Townley, F.D.Smith & J.A.Peden.
                                                      Runpast Publishing 1991.
The Industrial Railways of the Wigan Coalfield Part Two. C.H.A.Townley, F.D.Smith & J.A.Peden.
                                                     Runpast Publishing 1992
Clinker's Register of Closed Passenger Stations. C.R.Clinker. Avon-Anglia Publications 1988.
Signalling plans, Courtesy of Tony Graham, Tim Oldfield and Peter Hampson.
Manchester, Sheffield & Lincolnshire Plans, Courtesy of John Hall and Tony Graham.
Wigan Junction Railway Plans, Courtesy of John Ryan and Tim Oldfield.
Coal Mining in Lancashire & Cheshire, Alan Davies, Amberley Publishing 2010.
Various issues of The Leigh Chronicle and The Wigan Observer.
The Mancunian c1984.
The Manchester Guardian c1880-1900.

ABBREVIATIONS

B.R.	British Railways
C.L.C	Cheshire Lines Committee
C.WT.	Hundredweight
D.M.U.	Diesel Multiple Unit
G.C.R	Great Central Railway
L.C.G.B.	Locomotive Club of Great Britain
L.M.S.	London, Midland & Scottish Railway
L.N.E.R.	London North Eastern Railway
L.N.W.R	London & North Western Railway
L.U.R.	Lancashire Union Railway
L&Y.	Lancashire & Yorkshire Railway
M.o.D.	Ministry of Defence
M.R.	Midland Railway
M.S&L.R.	Manchester, Sheffield & Lincolnshire Railway
N.C.B.	National Coal Board
P.B.J.R.	Platt Bridge Junction Railway
P.W.	Permanent Way
R.E.C.	Railway Executive Committee
R.O.F.	Royal Ordnance Factory
S.B.	Signal Box
U.K.	United Kingdom
S.L.S.	Stephenson Locomotive Society
W.C.M.L.	West Coast Main Line
W.D.	War Department
W.T.T.	Working Time Table
W.W.II.	World War II.

Imperial to Metric conversion

1in (inch) = 25.4mm.
1ft (foot) = 304.8mm.
1yd (yard) = .944 metres. (22yds = 1 chain).
1 statute mile = 1.6093 kilometers.
1 acre* (4,870 sq yds) = .4097 hectares.
20 cwt (hundredweight) = 1 ton = 1.016 tonnes.